Images of ROYAL KENT

Cathy Tyce

Images of
ROYAL KENT

Cathy Tyce

First published in Great Britain by The Breedon Books Publishing Company Limited, Breedon House, 44 Friar Gate, Derby, DE1 1DA., 1998.

Reprint published in 2011 in Great Britain by The Derby Books Publishing Company Limited, 3 The Parker Centre, Mansfield Road, Derby, DE21 4SZ.

ISBN 978-1-908234-52-0

Printed and bound by Melita Press, Malta.

CONTENTS

Acknowledgements

I would like to express my gratitude to Linda Evans, of the Kent Messenger Group's Central Information Unit, and Julia Tompkins, of the Photographic Department, for their assistance in locating photographs for this publication. My thanks also go to my husband, Ian, for his support.

INTRODUCTION

PICTURE the scene. Gravesend in 1863 at the heart of the Victorian era. A love scene is about to be enacted before the eyes of the waiting populace. The future King Edward VII is coming to greet his bride, Princess Alexandra of Denmark, as she arrives in England for their wedding.

The town is in a frenzy at the honour of welcoming the future Queen. Committees have been set up to discuss everything from what gift to buy the bride to the clothes to be worn by the girls chosen to strew flowers in the Princess's path.

At last the great day arrives and the Royal Yacht *Victoria and Albert* berths at Terrace Pier. The bride appears on deck.

To the amazement of the waiting crowd the Prince abandons ceremony, springs on board and imprints a warm kiss on her glowing cheek.

The thousands of people who have turned out to play their own little part in the royal wedding celebrations are delighted at this totally unexpected display of affection. They cheer the gallant Prince – and the blushing bride beats a hasty retreat to her cabin.

We've always enjoyed a bit of romance, especially when it involves a Prince and Princess. As we have seen, Prince Charles and Princess Diana were by no means the first royal couple whose wedding sparked nationwide celebrations.

When the future King George V married Princess May of Teck in 1893, the Ashford MP gave £50 to pay for entertainment and tea for 2,000 children. In Rochester there was a grand firework display and in New Romney poorhouse inmates had a better dinner than usual.

King George V was the first King to broadcast wireless messages to the nation, the first whose voice was heard by all the people, the first whom they felt they knew.

And he was immensely popular. Here in Kent his 69th birthday parade in 1934 was watched by 4,000 people in the pouring rain at Shorncliffe, Folkestone.

His Silver Jubilee in 1935 was celebrated with bonfires, tableaux, a 21-gun salute at Folkestone and even a day off work for convicts in Maidstone prison. Tunbridge Wells was named the second best decorated provincial town in the country for the Jubilee.

When the King died, just a few months later, the Vicar of Maidstone, the Rev O.A.Standen, said: "We feel that we have lost the father of the family. We loved him and he loved us."

An echo from the past, of the feeling of loss felt by so many when Diana, Princess of Wales died in 1997.

Here in Kent we have long felt close to the royal family and enjoyed their visits.

They have touched every facet of life in the county: opened factories, visited schools, colleges, hospitals and churches, paid tribute to the work of the armed forces and the emergency services, supported charities and county organisations, brought comfort in times of war and hardship.

Some members of the family have special links with the county – for example, the Queen Mother as Lord Warden of the Cinque Ports, the Duchess of Kent as patron of the Friends of Rochester Cathedral and of the Royal British Legion Village, Aylesford, Princess Alexandra as patron of the Leeds Castle Foundation.

Others were at school here: Princess Diana at West Heath, Sevenoaks, Princess Anne at Benenden, Princes William and Richard, sons of the Duke and Duchess of Gloucester, at Wellesley House School, Broadstairs.

They have friends here, they come here to relax. Queen Victoria's son, the Duke of Edinburgh, lived at Eastwell Park, near Ashford, for many years. Prince Charles, more briefly, was resident in Chevening House, Sevenoaks, in the 1970s.

A former Lord Lieutenant of Kent, Marquis Camden, persuaded many members of the royal family to plant trees on the lawn of his home at Bayham Abbey, Lamberhurst. This royal grove included trees planted by Edward VII, George V, Queen Mary, Edward VIII, the Duke of Kent, the Duke of Cambridge and the Duke of Gloucester.

George V played golf in Deal, and Edward VII and the Duke of Windsor both played in Sandwich. George VI often went duck shooting at Grove Ferry between Canterbury and Thanet, sleeping on the royal train in a siding at the station.

Queen Victoria, daughter of an earlier Duke and Duchess of Kent, spent many childhood holidays in Ramsgate and Broadstairs and was often seen playing on the sands or the pier.

As a teenager she also visited Tunbridge Wells, staying with her mother at Calverley House, now the Calverley Hotel. They rode daily on the common, promenaded the Pantiles and took the springs.

Her last journey through Kent came in 1899 when she embarked for France from Folkestone. People seized vantage points along the railway line, hoping to catch a glimpse of the old Queen.

But they were disappointed and not a little hurt to see that she had pulled the blinds down in her carriage. It later emerged that the Queen had not intended an insult – it was simply that the sun was getting in her eyes.

Kent's position at the gateway to the continent meant many of our monarchs passed through on their way to and from wars, or foreign trips.

King Charles II landed at Dover in May 1660 after years of exile and made his way through Kent to London where he was crowned.

Another royal bride who arrived in Kent was Princess Marina of Greece who landed at Dover in November 1934 on her way to marry Prince George, the newly-created Duke of Kent.

There had been great jubilation in Kent when George V conferred the title, Duke of Kent, on his fourth son.

Feelings were so strong there had even been suggestions that the county council should petition the King to persuade him to confer the Kent title, but in the end no petition was needed.

Prince George already had many links with Kent. He went to school at St Peter's Court, Thanet, and had close friends here, including Sir Adrian and Lady Baillie, of Leeds Castle.

The Duke and Duchess quickly became great favourites in Kent. He became patron of the Association of Men of Kent and Kentish Men, of the Friends of Rochester Cathedral and other organisations and Colonel-in-Chief of the Queen's Own Royal West Kent Regiment.

The couple were seen to be hard-working and dedicated to their county, and to have a friendly, informal touch which endeared them to people. That was particularly noticeable when the Duke visited Ramsgate and Canterbury during the war after heavy bombing raids.

Sadly, the Duke was killed in action in August 1942 in a flying accident in Scotland.

But his widow and later their children, the present Duke of Kent, Princess Alexandra and Prince Michael of Kent, maintained their close links with the county.

There has been much discussion in recent years, intensified since the death of Diana, Princess of Wales, about the changing role and style of the royal family in this less deferential age.

Many of the changes can be seen in the photographs in this book. Royal visits have become more relaxed and friendly over the years, the settings less formal, the situations less forced.

But the one constant throughout these pictures is the obvious pride and pleasure the people in them have taken in welcoming royal visitors to our county.

Industry, Transport & Miscellaneous Duties

THE Queen and French President François Mitterrand officially opened the Channel Tunnel in October 1994. The ceremony marked one of the most significant developments in Kent's history – the creation of the first land link between the county and its continental neighbours.

Many of the pictures in this chapter mark important landmarks in our county's story – the opening of the Queen Elizabeth II bridge between Kent and Essex, the opening of Ashford International Station which brought the continent much closer to us, the opening of the Kingsferry Bridge linking Sheppey to the mainland, the launch of the hovercraft service to France, the opening of the Thamesport container and cargo port on the Isle of Grain.

Others are perhaps of less countywide importance but nonetheless demonstrate the onward march of Kent's economic development – the opening of factories, offices, shopping centres, civic centres, law courts, housing estates and tourist attractions.

Members of the royal family have also opened old people's homes, visited research centres, museums, collieries, railways, planted trees and unveiled statues.

Some visits have shown their caring side – for example in 1953 when both the Queen and the Duchess of Kent brought comfort to the people of North Kent whose homes had been devastated by floods.

And in 1972 the Duke of Edinburgh welcomed Asian refugees who had been thrown out of Uganda by President Idi Amin.

Other visits showed our respect for the royal family – for example when Prince Charles was given the honorary freedom of the city of Canterbury in 1978.

But what they all demonstrate is the diversity of the royal family's involvement in Kent life.

August 1926: The Duke of York, later King George VI, took a trip on the New Romney, Hythe and Dymchurch Railway which was nearing completion. He was shown round by Captain Howey, proprietor and promoter of the railway, and Mr H.Greenley, engineer and manager. The Duke, pictured here with Captain Howey, drove the Northern Engine over almost three miles of 15 inch track. He was on his annual visit to his camp at Jesson, Dymchurch, which was attended by 400 boys, half from public schools and half from factories and workshops.
Picture: *Topical Press Agency.*

October 1926: The Duke and Duchess of York, who would later become King George VI and Queen Elizabeth, visited the Southern Railway Company Works at Ashford. The Duchess, on her first official visit to the county, mounted the plate of the Lord Nelson engine, which her husband then drove to Ashford Station. The visit was a significant one for Ashford: the Duke switched on the town's electricity supply and the Duchess laid the foundation stone of Ashford Hospital. James Hogg, chairman of Ashford Urban Council, is seen introducing John Creery, clerk of the council, to the royal guests.

November 1926: The Prince of Wales cut the ribbon to open the West Cliff Promenade and Undercliffe at Ramsgate. He planted a tree then took a walk along the prom. Picture: *Topical Press Agency.*

July 1928: The Prince of Wales opened the Tunbridge Wells playing field donated to the town by Mr E.J.Strange, JP. The Prince went on to visit the Diamond Jubilee Show of Tunbridge Wells and South Eastern Counties Agricultural Society.

Picture: *Topical Press Agency.*

May 1934: The Duke of York showed a keen interest when he helped the horticultural research station at East Malling celebrate its 21st birthday on Empire Day, May 24. He saw how the station was trying to propagate the best walnut trees in Britain and inspected its work on pest eradication. He toured an 18-acre kiln orchard recently acquired by the station and started up a spraying machine.

December 1935: Elizabeth, Duchess of York, became the first royal visitor to Tenterden for 300 years when she performed the opening ceremony at the new home of the United Services Training Centre at St Michael's Grange. The centre had been set up in Loose, Maidstone, in May 1934 to train men to become cooks, housemen, handymen and the like. The scheme was so successful at getting men into work that the Ministry of Labour stepped in with extra cash and a grant for each trainee which enabled the centre to move into new premises and expand.

September 1936: Queen Mary paid her last visit to Kent, visiting a housing estate at Folkestone with local MP Sir Philip Sassoon.

June 1936: Prince George, Duke of Kent, took a stroll across Eynsford Bridge over the River Darent with parish council chairman Mrs J.Wood. While he was in the village he saw a tableau presented by the Women's Institute.

July 1936: The Duchess of Kent spent a day in Maidstone, visiting the British Legion Village, the Dunk Memorial Hall, headquarters of the Maidstone and District Corps of the St John Ambulance Brigade, and the Old Palace where she saw the work of the Maternity and Infant Clinic. She was then driven past cheering crowds to the Foster Clark estate where Mrs Booth, wife of timekeeper G.S.Booth, who was employed by Maidstone and District Bus company, showed her round her council house. The Duchess also visited the West Kent General Hospital and the Ophthalmic Hospital.

May 1938: These youngsters turned out to catch a glimpse of the Duke of Kent outside Hawkhurst Cottage Hospital. He had stopped off in the village as part of an extensive tour of the county. He visited the British Legion Club and unveiled commemorative heraldic panels at the King George V Playing Fields and a plate in memory of Mr M.J.Hardcastle who gave the field to the village.

Members of Brabourne WI bid a smiling farewell to the Duke as he left the village hall.

June 1939: These miners met the Duke of Kent when he dropped in at Snowdown Colliery during a day's tour of East Kent. He took great interest in the welfare of the miners and asked questions about soap, towels and clothing at the pithead baths. At Aylesham he took a red carnation from his buttonhole and gave it to a miner's wife. The Duke also visited Nonington, Wingham and Broadstairs where he went to Pierremont Hall, headquarters of the urban district council. Queen Victoria used to stay there when

visiting the town. He opened the 40-acre Northdown Park at Margate and visited St Gabriel's Convalescent Home, Westbrook, a Roman Catholic home for 45 delicate children.

The Duke opened the first section of Ramsgate's ARP tunnel system and was given a demonstration of gas masks.

This elderly resident of the 900-year-old St Bart's Hospital, at Sandwich, was introduced to the Duke.

November 1946: Princess Elizabeth made a private visit to Maidstone as the guest of Sir Garrard and Lady Tyrwhitt Drake. She visited Sir Garrard's zoo at Cobtree Manor and the Museum of Coaches and Carriages at the Old Tithe Barn in the town where she saw a travelling chariot used by King George III. At the zoo she was particularly interested in the cream ponies, descendants of those used at Windsor by Queen Victoria. The Princess walked across the road from the museum to visit All Saints' Church.

May 1950: Princess Margaret named a road after herself on her first official visit to Ramsgate. She visited the Newington housing estate and named its central thoroughfare, Princess Margaret Avenue. She then planted a commemorative tree. The Princess also cut the first sod on the site of the council's 1,000th post-war house.

February 1953: The worst floods in living memory hit Kent, bringing havoc and unparalleled damage to the county. The Duchess of Kent visited Sheerness to find out how people were faring. The week after the disaster the Queen crossed the Thames from Purfleet to Gravesend in a Port of London Authority launch to see the damage in North Kent. She was the first reigning monarch to make an official visit to Gravesend in 95 years. She talked to so many stricken residents that she was two hours behind schedule by the time she set off for Erith and Belvedere.

April 1955: The Queen and Prince Philip were shown around the refinery at the Isle of Grain by its general manager, C.S.Cleverley.

April 1957: The Duke of Edinburgh toured Reed Paper Group's site at Aylesford, visiting all its associated industries, including Kimberly-Clark Ltd and Reed Corrugated Cases. He is seen here talking to an operator in the stitching machine room at Medway Paper Sacks.

He also visited the East Malling Research Station where he toured the orchards sitting on a bale of straw in a farm trailer. Here he is seen with Elizabeth Keepe who was explaining the experiments being carried out to develop thornless gooseberries.

April 1960: Princess Marina, Duchess of Kent, opened the Kingsferry Bridge linking the Isle of Sheppey to the mainland and launched hopes of new progress and prosperity for the island. The bridge, completed in 27 months at a cost of £1.3 million, was decorated with a ton of bunting for the ceremony. The Duchess pressed a button, the traffic lights on the approach to the bridge flashed their warning and the 465-ton pastel green structure moved silently up the four supporting towers to the cheers of thousands of people lining the approach roads. The Duchess told the waiting crowds: "With the new railway and approach road it will make Sheppey far more attractive to both visitors and industrialists but because it is still an island it will lose none of its character."

May 1967: Princess Alexandra, daughter of the late Duke of Kent and Princess Marina, Duchess of Kent, signed this picture of herself after opening the £500,000 Civic Centre at Folkestone. The picture was to be hung in the eight-storey centre which was the tallest building in town. The Princess is pictured here with the Mayor of Folkestone, Cllr E.A.Lamb, and the town clerk, Mr N.Scragg.

May 1967: The Duke of Edinburgh flew out of Biggin Hill Air Show at the controls of a helicopter of the Queen's Flight.

July 1968: Princess Margaret had a wave for the crowds when she launched the world's first international hovercraft service. The Princess unveiled a plaque at the Dover hoverport which had been built on land reclaimed from the sea. She then travelled from Dover to Boulogne in Seaspeed's giant Mountbatten hovercraft SRN4 in just 37 minutes.

November 1968: Gravesend's £1 million Civic Centre was officially opened by the Duchess of Kent in the presence of the Mayor, Alderman Charles Suter. The Bishop of Rochester, Dr Richard Say, dedicated the centre. Afterwards the Duchess chatted to some of the many schoolchildren waiting outside.

October 1969: Princess Anne named the second of British Rail's Seaspeed hovercraft after herself at Dover. She unveiled a nameplate, signed a portrait of herself inside the terminal building then took a 30 minute trip on the hovercraft to the Goodwin Sands and back.

August 1972: The £2.5 million harbour extension at Sheerness was opened by Princess Alexandra. After unveiling a plaque she paid tribute to Kent's important role in the maritime history of the country. She is seen here with Medway Ports Authority chairman Maurice Gill who introduced her to the captain of one of the ships berthed in the harbour.

November 1972: Madhvi Pattni showered the Duke of Edinburgh with rose petals and rice in a traditional Indian welcome to the Uganda Resettlement Centre in West Malling. Mrs Pattni was one of the Asians expelled from Uganda by President Idi Amin. The Duke was the first member of the royal family to visit any of the resettlement camps set up for the families when they arrived in the United Kingdom.

May 1973: *Great Britain II*, the £100,000 Sandwich-built yacht of round-the-world sailor Chay Blyth, was launched by Princess Anne at Ramsgate.

April 1977: Prince Charles planted a copper beech sapling at Chevening, near Sevenoaks, the property which had been left to the nation by its previous owner, Lord Stanhope. Prince Charles lived there for a number of years. It is now the official residence of the Foreign Secretary. The beech tree was one of a dozen presented to the Prince by the Kent branch of the Men of the Trees. That evening he hosted a dinner at Chevening in aid of the Queen's Silver Jubilee Appeal.

May 1977: The Duke of Kent learned some of the finer points of loudspeaker manufacture from KEF Electronics managing director Raymond Cooke and staff member Joan Bottle. He was touring the factory at Tovil, Maidstone, as part of an export campaign in his role as vice chairman of the British Overseas Trade Board.

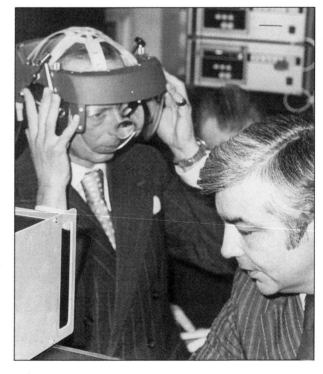

November 1977: The Duke of Kent tried on a pilot's head up display unit in the airborne display unit of Marconi Elliott Avionic Systems in Rochester. Also in the picture is marketing executive Dave Hussey.

June 1978: The ancient Royal Chapel at Leeds Castle was reconsecrated by the Archbishop of Canterbury, Dr Donald Coggan, after a 400 year gap in worship. Princess Alexandra, patron of the Leeds Castle Foundation, was there to mark the occasion, which took place on the feast day of St Augustine, first Archbishop of Canterbury.

November 1978: Huge crowds gathered to welcome Prince Charles to Canterbury to receive the honorary freedom of the city a week before his 30th birthday. He is seen here with the Archbishop of Canterbury, Dr Donald Coggan, Mrs Coggan, the High Sheriff of Kent, Major Ion Calvocoressi, and the Mayor of Canterbury, Cllr Dick Peard.

November 1978: Maidstone's traffic problems eased with the opening of the £2.5 million St Peter's Bridge across the River Medway by the Duke of Kent. The Duke is seen here being shown the riverside improvements by county surveyor Allen Smith. He also visited the Reed Group's de-inking plant at Aylesford and Key Terrain's injection moulding and extrusion factories and dined at County Hall, Maidstone, becoming the first royal visitor to be entertained there.

May 1979: Guides and Cubs were among the thousands of people who welcomed the Queen Mother to Chatham for the official opening of the £8.5 million administrative headquarters of Lloyds of London in Dock Road.

July 1979: Edward and Lilian Cansdale were proud to welcome the Queen Mother to their flat in the Royal British Legion's Queen Mother Court in Borstal Road, Rochester. The Queen Mother officially opened the 60 old people's flats, wishing all the tenants true peace and happiness.

She took a closer view of the River Medway through a pair of binoculars lent by one of the tenants, Moss Noah.

October 1979: The mysteries of cement making were explained to the Duke of Kent during a visit to see a £25 million extension to the Rugby Portland Cement company's complex in Halling.

May 1982: The Port of Sheerness was packed with well-wishers when Princess Margaret arrived to name the Olau Line's huge ferry, the Olau Britannia. She pulled the lever on a brass ship's telegraph which tugged a rope to unhitch the bottle which crashed into the vessel's side.

May 1983: Princess Diana captivated the hearts of people in Kent on her first official visit to the county. About 35,000 people turned out to welcome her to Canterbury where she officially opened Cranmer House, warden-assisted flats for the elderly in London Road. As patron of the Pre-School Playgroups' Association she had asked to meet members of local playgroups so about 80 children and leaders were there to see her. The Princess paid a private visit to the cathedral where she opened a lift for the disabled.

December 1983: Claire Jackson, seven, had a royal helping hand at the official opening of Ashford Council's Civic Centre in Tannery Lane. Claire, daughter of the council's principal assistant engineer, held tightly on to the Duchess of Kent's hand as she toured the housing and treasurer's departments.

April 1984: Huge crowds turned out to say goodbye to the Queen Mother after she spent a day in the Medway Towns. She visited the Arethusa Venture Centre in Lower Upnor in her role as its patron. The centre offers fun breaks to underprivileged young people from London and other urban areas. The Queen Mother also visited the Sir John Hawkins Hospital in Chatham High Street to see its £200,000 facelift.

October 1984: The Queen opened the Law Courts on the riverside at Maidstone and spoke of her regret that an increase in criminal jurisdiction and in civil and matrimonial disputes made them necessary. She is pictured here with Judge John Streeter, Kent's senior circuit judge.

October 1984: The Queen delighted the crowds in Rochester High Street during a tour of the Medway Towns which included visits to the Molly Wisdom Hospice, Rochester's Corn Exchange, Chatham Dockyard and Gillingham Business Park.

May 1985: With a flourish, the Duke of Gloucester named a diesel locomotive on the Romney, Hythe and Dymchurch Railway. He unfurled the banner of Southlands School, New Romney, to reveal a plaque bearing the name, John Southland, the man who founded the school in 1610. The Duke climbed into the cab of the loco and, with a bit of help from chief engineer Tony Crowhurst, drove it from Hythe to New Romney. From there he went to Lydd to unveil a plaque to open an exhibition marking the town's centenary.

September 1985: These patriotic runners greeted the Duchess of Kent when she opened a controlled atmosphere store at East Kent Packers Ltd, Faversham. The team presented her with a cheque for £150 for the Helen House Hospice. They had raised the money in charity races.

September 1986: Radio Kent sports reporter Duncan Jones met Princess Alexandra when she opened the station's £1.5 million studios at Sun Pier, Chatham. The Princess stopped to talk to so many people her visit overran by 20 minutes. Station manager Mike Marsh said the visit had been a happy, informal occasion.

October 1987: Staff of Rodenstock UK Ltd donned Bavarian costume to welcome Princess Michael of Kent when she opened the company's high-tech optical plant at Springhead Enterprise Park, Northfleet.

June 1988: The Duke of Gloucester was given a demonstration of warfare in the Napoleonic age when he visited Fort Amherst at Chatham. He toured the underground tunnels in the fort which was one of a number built to protect Chatham Dockyard from French attack. Members of the Fort Amherst and Lines Trust which owns the site, manned the ramparts and fired a replica cannon to show how the militia would have warded off any attack.

May 1989: There was a carnival atmosphere in Whitstable when the Prince of Wales dropped by as part of a whirlwind tour of East Kent. His day also included visits to Canterbury and Faversham where he made a tour of inspection of Brogdale experimental fruit farm which was then under threat of closure.

September 1990: Princess Anne had a go behind the wheel when she opened Thamesport, the container and cargo port on the Isle of Grain.

November 1990: The Queen Mother, Lord Warden of the Cinque Ports, paid tribute to a former holder of the office when she unveiled a bronze statue of Sir Winston Churchill and his wife Lady Churchill at his former home, Chartwell, near Westerham. The house is now owned by the National Trust, of which the Queen Mother is president. The ceremony marked the 50th anniversary of Churchill becoming Prime Minister and the 25th anniversary of his death.

May 1991: Princess Anne and Dover District Council chairman Paul Watkins came face to face with Corporal Crabbe and Sid Seagull, alias South Kent College student Myles Kearney, when she opened the White Cliffs Experience at Dover. She spent more than an hour touring the £14 million heritage centre.

July 1991: Princess Alexandra opened paper manufacturer Whatman's £6 million complex on the 20/20 Estate at Allington, near Maidstone. She was presented with a bouquet by six-year-old Helen Wright. Whatman, which was founded in Maidstone in 1740, made paper which was used by Queen Victoria for writing letters and by Napoleon Bonaparte for his will. In 1993 the Princess's brother, The Duke of Kent, visited Whatman's Springfield Mill paper plant in Maidstone to launch a £4.2 million machine that was named after him. It continued a Whatman tradition of naming each new machine after a royal duke. The others were named York, Edinburgh and Cornwall.

July 1991: Princess Alexandra took to a golf buggy during a charity tournament at Leeds Castle. The Princess, seen here with Lord Aldington, chairman of the Leeds Castle Foundation, watched blind golfers and celebrities such as Colin Cowdrey and commentator Brian Moore play on the castle's course. The event was organised to mark the Guide Dogs for the Blind Association's 60th anniversary. The Princess is patron of both the GDBA and the Leeds Castle Foundation.

October 1991: A long-awaited moment for commuters between Kent and Essex. The Queen officially opened the £86 million Thames bridge at Dartford by unveiling a monument on the Essex side. Its name – a not very well-kept secret until then – was revealed to be the Queen Elizabeth II Bridge.

October 1992: The Royal Victoria Place Shopping Centre in Tunbridge Wells had a royal opening ceremony to match its royal name. Thousands of well-wishers lined the streets and packed into the centre hoping to catch a glimpse of Princess Diana who unveiled a plaque to mark the opening of the £100 million centre.

May 1993: The Prince of Wales joined a group of children from Kent Watch groups who were pond dipping at Tyland Barn, headquarters of Kent Trust for Nature Conservation, at Sandling, near Maidstone. The restoration work to the 17th-century barn had finished only at 7.15 the previous evening and some of the brickwork mortar was still wet when the Prince arrived for the official opening.

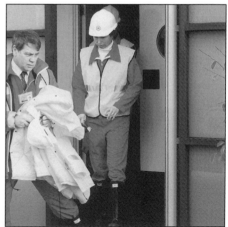

October 1993: Princess Anne donned red overalls, a reflective jacket, safety boots and a hard hat when she toured the Eurotunnel Exhibition Centre and Channel Tunnel Terminal at Cheriton as president of the Chartered Institute of Transport.

May 1994: Great Britain was an island no more. The Queen boarded a Eurostar train at Waterloo International and travelled across Kent and through the Channel Tunnel to meet French President François Mitterrand in Calais for the first of two official opening ceremonies for the Channel Tunnel. Both then returned to Kent on board Le Shuttle for the inauguration ceremony at the Folkestone terminal.

February 1996: Kent's links with the continent took a giant leap forward with the opening of the £100 million Ashford International Station which allowed passengers for the first time to take a train direct to Paris or Brussels and arrive within a couple of hours. The Duke of Kent travelled by train from London with Transport Secretary Sir George Young for the opening ceremony. Customer care worker Maria Lawrence is pictured explaining to the Duke how to book a ticket.

November 1994: Abbott Laboratories in Queenborough on the Isle of Sheppey wanted there to be no confusion about who their royal guest was so they gave the Queen a white coat with her name on. During her visit, to congratulate the company on winning the Queen's Award for Industry, she was shown its latest healthcare product, a new type of antibiotic.

Hospitals & Emergency Services

CHARTING royal visits to hospitals in Kent over the last 60 years or so is almost like reading an uplifting history of healthcare in the county. Hospitals opened or facilities improved at Ashford, Tunbridge Wells, Folkestone, Canterbury, Maidstone, Rochester, Benenden, Pembury, Dartford, Faversham and Margate.

Each time, a royal visitor marked the occasion.

Then the hospice movement developed, and that, too, began to attract royal sympathy and support in Kent.

The Queen officially opened the Molly Wisdom Hospice in Rochester and Princess Diana opened the Heart of Kent Hospice in Aylesford.

Each royal visitor took the time to talk not only to patients but also to nurses, doctors and other workers to mark their recognition of the dedication of healthcare staff.

But they have also shown their appreciation of the police, the fire service and all other emergency services in the county.

Kent, with its long coastline and busy sea channels, particularly values The Royal National Lifeboat Institution, whose volunteers have saved so many lives.

Several members of the royal family, including the Queen Mother, who is patron of the RNLI, have visited lifeboat stations here over the years – to celebrate an anniversary or to name a new boat.

Just a couple of months after she became Lord Warden of the Cinque Ports in 1979 the Queen Mother was back in Dover to name a new vessel. At the age of 79 she managed to shrug off the effects of a cold, wet November morning and chat happily to the lifeboatmen. It is a day they will long remember.

July 1921: The Prince of Wales spent a day in Kent visiting Dover, Deal, Folkestone and Maidstone. He unveiled a memorial to the Dover Patrol, at St Margaret's Bay, and visited Preston Hall at Aylesford, where he chatted to patients. Here he is pictured in Folkestone where he laid the foundation stone of the nurses' home at the hospital. He is talking to the mayoress, wife of the Mayor, Alderman R.G. Wood, at Radnor Park. The following day he visited HMS *Worcester* at Greenhithe and the Glentworth Club in Dartford.

July 1930: The Prince of Wales flew from London to Swingate, near Dover, on his way to name the new £18,430 Dover lifeboat, the *Sir William Hillary*, the world's largest lifeboat. It was named after the founder of the Royal National Lifeboat Institution.

As he arrived in the dock members of the British Legion formed a guard of honour.

July 1932: The Duchess of York, the future Queen Elizabeth, laid the foundation stone of the hospital at Tunbridge Wells which was to combine the existing General Hospital and the Eye and Ear Hospital. Later that day she visited the Tunbridge Wells and South Eastern Counties Agricultural Society's 64th annual show.

July 1935: The foundation stone of the Kent and Canterbury Hospital at Canterbury was laid by the Duke of Kent. He is seen here passing along the ranks of the Women's Section of the British Legion with the Mayor of Canterbury, Alderman Frank Wood, on his way to the site.

July 1937: Almost exactly two years later the Duke of Kent returned with his wife to open the hospital. The couple flew into Manston Aerodrome on their way to Canterbury.

The Duke and Duchess made their way past the nurses lined up to welcome them to the £150,000 hospital which, the Duke said, did honour to Canterbury. He added that he was impressed at the way new features had been made possible by the use of reinforced concrete. Mr W.K.Whigham, president of the hospital, thanked all the people of the city and surrounding villages who had raised the funds to make the hospital a reality. After the ceremony a Daimler ambulance, donated by Canon and Mrs Livett, was driven round the courtyard to loud cheers. Later the Duchess wrote the words 'Marina, July 14th, 1937' in a slab of wet concrete. The Duke had done the same thing at the foundation stone laying. The two slabs were incorporated in the front of the building. The Duke and Duchess went on to the Kent County Agricultural Show at Canterbury.

May 1946: The centenary of the Kent County Ophthalmic and Aural Hospital at Maidstone was celebrated with a visit by its patron, the Duchess of Kent. She attended a thanksgiving service in neighbouring Holy Trinity Church and had lunch at the Royal Star Hotel in the town where 100 guests were invited to meet her. She is pictured talking to one of the patients, nine-month-old Frances Chapman.

July 1950: Queen Elizabeth became the first Queen since Elizabeth I to visit Cranbrook. She was on her way to Benenden Sanatorium where a crowd of 2,500 people gathered on the lawn to greet her. The Queen chatted to patients as she toured the new medical unit. She then left for Tenterden.

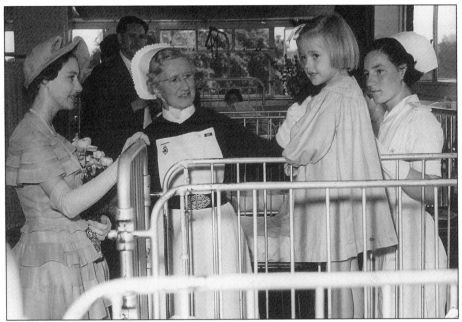

July 1952: Monica Ellenden, three, had a royal visitor while she was a patient at the Royal Victoria Hospital, Folkestone. Princess Margaret toured children's wards, medical and surgical wards and a new wing built to replace one destroyed by German shellfire during the war. She also visited the Bruce Porter Home for invalid children where she unveiled a plaque beside a lift given to the home by the people of Folkestone and Hythe. She had tea at the Leas Cliff Hall.

March 1956: The Queen Mother paid a return visit to Benenden Sanatorium to mark the completion of a new wing on the 50th anniversary of the laying of the foundation stone. The 210-bed sanatorium was run by the Civil Service Society of which the Queen Mother was patron. Many of the patients were Post Office engineers who managed to rig up an ingenious relay system so that a room-to-room commentary could be made on the royal visit.

May 1956: The lifeboatmen of Walmer lined up to welcome the Queen Mother when she arrived at the station to present a certificate to mark its centenary. The same day she opened an accommodation block at the Royal Marines Depot at Deal. The massed bands of the Royal Marines School of Music played on the North Barracks Parade Ground as the royal guest arrived to inspect the 700 marines. It was the first time the Queen Mother had been to the depot but she recalled that her late husband had visited 27 years earlier as Duke of York.

June 1957: Princess Alexandra, daughter of the late Prince George, Duke of Kent, walked almost a mile through the ranks of more than 1,000 policemen from all over the county when she inspected a vast parade at County Police Headquarters, Maidstone. The plan had been for her to tour the ranks in a vehicle but she insisted on walking. It was the climax of a ceremony to mark the centenary of the Kent Constabulary. The Princess paid tribute to the force saying it had 'established a high place in the affections of all who live in the county and is universally respected and admired'.

July 1967: Princess Marina named the new Dover lifeboat, *Faithful Forester*. She is pictured talking to crew member T.Austin.

March 1969: Children of staff at the Kent and Sussex Hospital, Tunbridge Wells, had front row seats when the Duchess of Kent visited their day nursery. She toured the new ophthalmic department at the hospital and two wards before moving on to Pembury Hospital to open the maternity unit there.

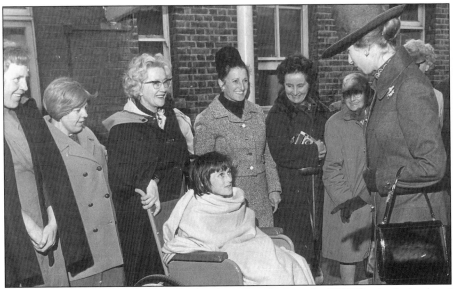

November 1971: Princess Anne met staff and patients when she opened a £500,000 outpatients wing at West Hill Hospital, Dartford.

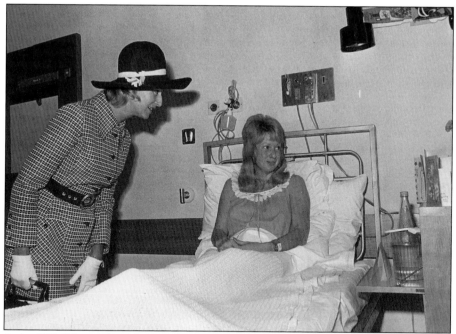

August 1972: Princess Alexandra chatted to a patient at the Kent and Canterbury Hospital, Canterbury, which her father, the Duke of Kent, officially opened 35 years earlier.

March 1977: Rose Rumena of Lamberhurst had a special guest at her 85th birthday party in Pembury Hospital Geriatric Assessment Unit. The Queen Mother made her day by cutting her birthday cake for her. She also opened the Florence Balls House for the elderly in Tunbridge Wells administered by the Distressed Gentlefolk's Aid Association.

May 1978: A smiling Princess Alexandra waved to staff as she visited St Bartholomew's Hospital, Rochester.

November 1979: Rain did not stop the Queen Mother smiling when she boarded Dover's new lifeboat, *Rotary Service*. The Queen Mother, patron of the Royal National Lifeboat Institution, officially named the vessel which was partly funded by Rotary International Great Britain and Ireland.

November 1979: Alf Manning, coxswain of the Ramsgate lifeboat, met Princess Margaret at the naming ceremony for the town's new lifeboat, *Silver Jubilee*.

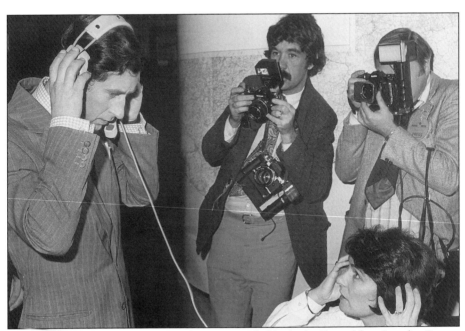

December 1979: Prince Charles made radio contact with ships in the Channel from Langdon Battery, the new coastguard station at Dover which he officially opened.

June 1984: Princess Alexandra found plenty to smile about when these nurses welcomed her to the official opening of the £20 million Maidstone Hospital. She spent so much time with patients as she toured the hospital that her visit ran well behind schedule.

September 1985: Leading Fireman Martin Fryer presented Princess Anne with a fireman's axe when she opened Tonbridge Fire Station. Earlier that day she had watched a mini-rugby match and unveiled a plaque at Tunbridge Wells Borderers Sports Club.

December 1985: Rachel Malic came face to face with the Princess of Wales at the William Harvey Hospital, Ashford. The Princess, as patron of the National Rubella Council, met women who had been vaccinated against German measles. She returned to the hospital in October 1992 to open the Paula Carr Diabetes Care Centre.

September 1986: Communications assistant Maureen Perrin took time out from her duties in the control room at Maidstone Police Station to talk to the Duchess of Kent. The Duchess performed the official opening ceremony of the station and magistrates court complex.

January 1989: The Duchess of Kent chatted to 84-year-old Ruth Harvey, of Boughton, after her husband, the Duke of Kent, had opened the 24-bed Kent wing of Faversham Cottage Hospital. Mrs Harvey remembered the Duke's father, Prince George, Duke of Kent, visiting the hospital in the 1930s.

October 1990: The Princess of Wales visited St Augustine's Psychiatric Hospital, Chartham, as patron of the charity, Turning Point, which helps those with drink, drug and mental health problems. She toured three wards and met patients before joining in a seminar on mental health.

July 1991: Fred Pain was delighted to receive a 79th birthday present of a posy from the Duchess of York when she visited the Molly Wisdom Hospice in Rochester.

October 1992: The Princess of Wales brought comfort to patients at the official opening of the Heart of Kent Hospice, Preston Hall, Aylesford. She had a friendly, relaxed chat with each of the patients and even had a hug for Gladys File, 67. Mrs File gave her a book about the life of Jesus, a gift from her grandsons to Princes William and Harry.

June 1996: Prince Charles opened Margate's hospital, named after his grandmother, the Queen Elizabeth the Queen Mother Hospital. Signed portraits of both the Queen Mother and the Prince of Wales have been given pride of place in the entrance hall. The Prince is seen here with physiotherapy patient Florence Hobson, 77, from Broadstairs.

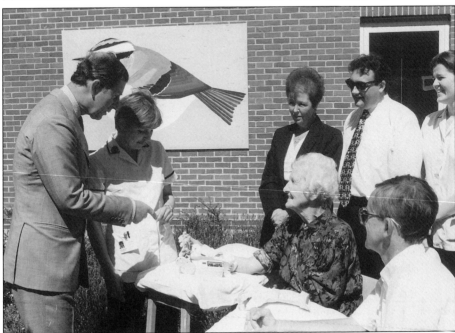

THE SERVICES AND THE WAR YEARS

WHEN Princess Diana visited the newly created Princess of Wales's Royal Regiment in Canterbury in 1993 she was continuing a long history of morale-building royal visits to troops in Kent.

Virtually every county branch of the Armed Forces, from cadet to veteran, has proudly paraded before a member of the royal family.

But some regiments have special royal links.

The Queen's Own Royal West Kent Regiment had two royal Colonels-in-Chief — first the Duke of Kent, then, after his death in 1942, his widow the Duchess of Kent, who quickly won the affection of the regiment.

The Buffs (Royal East Kent Regiment) were proud to have King Frederik IX of Denmark as their Colonel-in-Chief.

Those two famous Kent regiments amalgamated in 1961, then became part of The Queen's Regiment which in turn amalgamated with The Royal Hampshires to form The Princess of Wales's Royal Regiment.

Princess Diana was an immediate favourite with her regiment and its families. Many of the wives spoke after her death of her kindness to them and their children.

The Queen, too, enjoys a warm relationship with the regiments of which she is Colonel-in-Chief, among them The Royal Green Jackets, The Royal Engineers and The Argyll and Sutherland Highlanders, all of which she has visited in Kent.

The Queen Mother has had a special place in the hearts of the people since she and the King did such a fine job of keeping morale high during the war.

1926: King George V came down to Chatham to review the Royal Engineers. He arrived on the parade ground with the Officer Commanding, General Sir Bindon Blood.

The visit they paid to Folkestone and Dover in 1944 greatly cheered the people of those frontline towns.

And since the war the Queen Mother has not forgotten those who served – attending services to honour the Normandy veterans and to mark the 40th anniversary of Dunkirk.

The royal family has given tremendous support to ex-servicemen and women, too, through the Royal British Legion Village at Preston Hall, Aylesford, which the Legion took over in 1925 to provide treatment, homes and work for ex-servicemen with tuberculosis.

The Duke and Duchess of York were among early royal visitors, as was the Prince of Wales, the Legion's president. And in 1975, the Queen, patron of the Royal British Legion, toured the village during its 50th anniversary celebrations.

But undoubtedly its closest royal friend is the Duchess of Kent who became its first royal patron in 1980 and has been a regular, and much-loved visitor ever since.

October 1926: The Duke of York, the future King George VI, inspected a guard of honour formed by the 386th Field Battery of the Royal Artillery, when he arrived in Ashford.

November 1926: The Prince of Wales inspected The Buffs at Margate.

June 1929: The Prince of Wales, later King Edward VIII, was at Dover to inspect the 1st Battalion of the Seaforth Highlanders of which he was Colonel-in-Chief.

June 1929: Major General Sir Frederick Maurice, chairman of the council of management of the British Legion Village, Preston Hall, Aylesford, greeted the Duke and Duchess of York when they arrived at the village for a visit to the factories and workshops. The Duchess was presented with a monogrammed crocodile-skin case made at the factory by Mr S.G.Brown. The couple also visited Maidstone where they inspected 2,000 Boy Scouts, Wolf Cubs, Girl Guides and Brownies, at the Lock Meadows, as today's Lockmeadow was then known. Maidstone High Street was festooned with bunting and flags to welcome the Duke and Duchess as they drove to the Town Hall to receive a loyal address from the borough. They then went to Mote Park where thousands of legionnaires from all over the county were gathered for a huge British Legion rally.

June 1932: The Prince of Wales, newly-elected national president of the British Legion, visited Preston Hall, Aylesford, near Maidstone, where he was given a rapturous welcome by 5,000 legionnaires. He toured the sanatorium wards and the workshops in the industrial section then took the salute at a great march past of Legion members from 120 Kent branches. These Boy Scouts and Wolf Cubs greeted the Prince on his arrival. He is seen here accompanied by Sir Frederick Maurice.

July 1933: Prince George, who the following year would become Duke of Kent, visited the *Arethusa* at Upnor, near Rochester. He launched it on its career as a training ship for Britain's boy sailors.

June 1934: The Princess Royal inspected the 1st Battalion Royal Scots Regiment at Dover.

July 1935: The Prince of Wales visited the Duke of York's Royal Military School at Guston, Dover, to present new colours to the 2nd Battalion of the Seaforth Highlanders. Afterwards families had the chance to meet the regiment's Colonel-in-Chief.

July 1935: Recruit A.J.Payton was singled out for honour when the Prince of Wales visited the Royal Marines Depot at Dover later that day to inspect the 212th King's Squad before passing them out for duty in the corps. The Prince presented him with the King's badge for the smartest recruit.

November 1935: The Duke of Kent, Colonel-in-Chief of the Queen's Own Royal West Kent Regiment, paid his first visit to its Maidstone Depot. He is seen here with Major A.A.E.Chitty.

July 1936: Wounded war veteran Edward Clark presented a bouquet to the Duchess of Kent when she visited the British Legion Village, Preston Hall, Aylesford.

February 1940: King George VI received a tumultuous reception when he visited troops in the Medway Towns. Wearing the uniform of the Admiral of the Fleet, he spent the day inspecting detachments of the Royal Navy, Royal Marines and Royal Engineers and the work in progress at Chatham Dockyard.

April 1940: The King and Queen brought cheer to the troops when they visited East Kent. The King inspected defence preparations along the coast. Here he is seen at Shorncliffe, Folkestone.

The King drove on to Dover where he inspected troops at the Castle and was shown anti-aircraft devices.

The Queen inspected a Scottish Regiment of which she was Honorary Colonel.

May 1941: The Duke of Kent toured Civil Defence Services in Canterbury and Ashford including the Fire Brigade, the Auxiliary Fire Service, War Reserve and Special Constables and Women's Voluntary Service for Civil Defence.

June 1941: The King is seen leaving the XIIth Corps HQ in Tunbridge Wells with General Sir Bernard Paget and Field Marshal Lord Montgomery.

December 1941: The Duke of Kent visited a Kent war factory in his role as Inspector of Factories to see how women war workers were faring. The factory was not named in the *Kent Messenger* of the time, which reported that the Duke 'took a studious interest when he saw some 'hush-hush' activity'.

June 1942: The Duke of Kent spent two hours touring Canterbury after the devastating bombing raid by German aircraft. He spoke to many residents, ARP wardens and city officials, visited the British Restaurant where many of those who had been bombed out were being fed, and even accepted an invitation to have a beer in a 16th century inn damaged by a bomb. He left the city with the rousing words: "We shall win. Keep your chins up." He is seen here talking to women shop workers.

The Mayor of Canterbury showed the Duke the devastation. They are seen here outside St George's Church.

1943: After the death of her husband, the Duke of Kent, on active service in August 1942, Princess Marina, Duchess of Kent, continued to make many visits to the county. Here she is seen talking to nurses outside County Hall, Maidstone.

February 1943: Hundreds of Wrens saluted the Duchess of Kent, Commandant of the Women's Royal Naval Service, when she visited Chatham. Her first stop was at Admiralty House where she inspected officers and ratings and saw them at work. She moved on to the Dockyard where she inspected Wrens of the motor transport section. She was introduced to Wren Petty Officer Wanda Morgan from Whitstable, former women's open golf champion, who had joined the service 16 months earlier. The Duchess's visit ended at the Royal Naval Barracks where she talked to Wrens in their mess and resting rooms.

July 1943: The Duchess of Kent visited Combe Bank and Parkwood, two convalescent homes run by the County of Kent War Organisation of the British Red Cross Society and Order of St John Jerusalem. She toured wards and recreation rooms and talked to men engaged in occupational therapy.

October 1944: The same two convalescent homes had another royal visit, this time from the Princess Royal.

October 1944: The King and Queen toured Dover and Folkestone to meet the unsung heroes and heroines of those towns who had put up with four years of shelling, bombing and doodlebugs. They chatted with townsfolk about their grim experiences and saw the shattered houses and the air-raid shelters which were now the only home for many people. They also saw Winchelsea caves which served as sleeping quarters for many whose homes had been destroyed by enemy action. At Folkestone Sports Ground there was a delighted reception for the King and Queen who saw a huge parade of Civil Defence Services, the Land Army, hospital staff and many others who had helped in the war effort in these frontline towns. The Queen had a special smile for these men of the National Fire Service.

The Queen at Wardens Post Z4 on Dover Cliffs, the post nearest the enemy.

October 1944: The Duchess of Kent praised the work of the Wrens of the Dover Command when she visited them at Dover Castle.

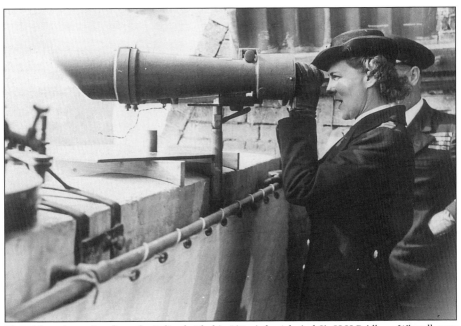

These binoculars, taken from the Italian battleship Littoria by Admiral Sir H.H.Pridham-Wippell, gave the Duchess the chance to look across the Channel from Dover and see the coastline of France, now freed from the Germans.

July 1945: At last the war in Europe was over and the work of these Land Girls, who had helped feed the country during those dark days, was finished. About 1,700 of them, smartly dressed in fawn breeches and green jumpers, paraded before the Duchess of Kent at the St Lawrence County Cricket Ground, Canterbury. Earlier they had filled Canterbury Cathedral for a service in their honour. The Duchess told them: "The really splendid work you have done during the war, entailing long and arduous hours with little rest has largely contributed to the great victory in Europe. We in this country are proud of you and thank you sincerely for the vital tasks you have performed on farms and in gardens which has helped the nation so much and will not be forgotten."

July 1948: The King visited the Royal Naval Barracks and Hospital at Gillingham and the recently opened NAAFI Services' Club at Brompton. It was the first NAAFI club in Britain to have residential accommodation for married personnel. The King spoke to Warrant Officer Newman, his wife and daughters, the first family to stay at the club. Also in the picture are Admiral Sir Harold M.Burrough and Sir Lancelot C.Royle.

November 1949: The Queen visited Biggin Hill, Kent's famous Battle of Britain fighter station to inspect the No 600 (City of London) Squadron, Royal Auxiliary Air Force of which she was Honorary Air Commodore. She addressed the squadron from the control tower then nine of the squadron's Spitfires took off for a spectacular display.

May 1952: The 151 men of the Kent Yeomanry who died in the war were commemorated on a memorial unveiled at All Saints' Church, Maidstone, by the Duchess of Kent. It was an addition to the 1914-18 memorial in the south wall of the church. The ceremony was witnessed by almost 1,000 relatives of the fallen men, and past and present members of the regiment with their wives and sweethearts.

April 1955: The Queen Mother took her first helicopter flight when she flew into Biggin Hill for a St George's Day ceremony.

May 1955: King Frederik IX of Denmark, Colonel-in-Chief of The Buffs, presented new Colours to the First Battalion of his regiment at the St Lawrence Cricket Ground in Canterbury.

July 1955: The Queen Mother and the Duchess of Gloucester spent four hours touring the WRAF Station at Hawkinge. Among the cadets they met were four pioneers of the Burmese Women's Air Force who were training at Hawkinge and who would return home to become the nucleus of officers to train the new Women's Air Force out there. The royal visitors watched a PT display and visited the station church of St Hugh of Lincoln.

October 1956: The Medway Towns gave a warm welcome to Queen Elizabeth II when she came to celebrate the centenary of the current corps of the Royal Engineers of which she is Colonel-in-Chief. She arrived by train at Meopham Station and drove to Rochester, cheered along the route by waiting crowds. She visited the Guildhall and cathedral in Rochester before driving on to Chatham Town Hall and Gillingham Municipal Buildings. The Queen finally arrived at Brompton Barracks, Gillingham, for the centenary celebrations. She also visited Gordon Barracks before driving to Gillingham to take the train back to London.

June 1957: Earl Mountbatten of Burma, Commodore of Sea Scouts, visited the Thames Nautical Training College, HMS *Worcester*, at Greenhithe. He handed a glass dish engraved with a picture of HMS *Worcester* and the Scouts Badge to Captain Gordon C.Steele, VC, Captain-Superintendent of the training college, to thank him for his kindness to London Sea Scouts who had been coming to camp in the college grounds for 10 years. Earl Mountbatten inspected 500 London Sea Scouts who had spent their Whitsun holiday there. He saw demonstrations of underwater swimming by boys of the 35th Westminster Sea Scouts, the first Sea Scout frogmen's unit in the country. The Earl was presented with the Broad Pennant of Commodore of the Sea Scouts by Major P.H.B.Wall, MP, Commissioner of Sea Scouts for London.

November 1957: The Duke of Edinburgh visited the Royal Marines Barracks at Deal, where he was shown the instrument repair shop. Musical instruments used by ships' bands all over the world were serviced and repaired there. The Duke also opened Deal's £250,000 pier.

July 1958: A service of thanksgiving was held at Canterbury Cathedral to mark the Golden Jubilee of the Territorial Army in Kent. Princess Marina attended the service with Lord Cornwallis, president of Kent Territorial and Auxiliary Forces' Association.

October 1958: The Duke of Kent, who had inherited the title on the death of his father in 1942, signed the visitors' book before leaving Ferryfield Airport, Lydd, on his way to join his regiment, the Royal Scots Greys, in Germany. He is pictured with Captain John Walton, adjutant, D.Kinnear, airport manager, and L.C.W. Turner, area traffic superintendent.

July 1959: A crowd of about 7,000 people gathered to greet Princess Marina Duchess of Kent when she launched the first of a new class of submarines, HMS *Oberon,* in Chatham Dockyard. It was the 52nd submarine to be built in the yard since the first in 1907. Admiral Superintendent Rear Admiral J.Y.Thompson presented the Duchess with a gift of her choice, a folding tea-table made in the yard, and with a picture painted by a dockyard draughtsman. The Duchess flew by helicopter to King's School, Rochester, where she inspected a guard of honour of members of the Army Cadet Corps, pictured here. She then went to Evensong at Rochester Cathedral, a service held in connection with the Friends of Rochester Cathedral of which she was patron.

July 1960: The Duchess of Kent, Colonel-in-Chief of the Queen's Own Royal West Kent Regiment, attended its final annual reunion before its amalgamation with The Buffs. A reunion service at All Saints' Church, Maidstone, was followed by a parade of past and present servicemen headed by the regimental band which made its way to the regimental war memorial at Brenchley Gardens. The Duchess took the salute at the march past at the Depot. She then visited the newly-housed regimental museum in St Faith's Street, pictured here.

November 1960: These boys demonstrated their knot-tying skills when the Duke of Edinburgh visited the training ship, *Arethusa*, at Upnor, near Rochester.

July 1962: The Queen and the Duke of Edinburgh marked the centenary of the Incorporated Thames Nautical Training College by going on board its floating school, HMS *Worcester* at Greenhithe, where the Queen presented a gold medal to the cadet with the qualities likely to make the finest sailor. The cadet chosen to receive the honour was Charles Talbut, 17, whose parents ran the White Horse Pub at Finglesham, Northbourne, near Deal. The royal couple were taken out to the *Worcester* on board the Port of London Authority's launch, *Nore*.

March 1968: The Queen spent three and a half hours on a private visit to the Royal School of Military Engineering at Brompton Barracks, Gillingham, in her role as Colonel-in Chief of the Royal Engineers. She and the Duke of Edinburgh looked at new buildings and saw the soldiers at work and leisure.

The Queen was delighted to see this huntsman and hounds.

November 1972: These binoculars were made for the Queen at the Royal Armament Research and Development Establishment at Fort Halstead, near Sevenoaks, and presented to her by its director, F.H.East. The Queen met apprentices and staff and saw some of the armaments in the Test House.

Apprentice of the year Graham Ayers, 21, of Sidcup, was introduced to the Queen. The Duke of Edinburgh is seen talking to Brian Clough, 19, of Swanley.

December 1972: While serving in the Royal Navy Prince Charles arrived at Chatham Naval Base on board the frigate HMS *Minerva* which had been fog-bound for two days in the Medway off Sheerness. The Prince, a Sub-Lieutenant, spent Christmas at Windsor before returning to Chatham to set sail on the *Minerva* on the first leg of a voyage to the West Indies.

August 1973: The Duchess of Kent paid her first visit to Shorncliffe Barracks at Folkestone to inspect the Junior Infantrymen's Battalion Passing Out Parade.

July 1975: The Queen visited the Royal Green Jackets at Connaught Barracks, Dover, as the regiment's Colonel-in-Chief. At Fort Burgoyne, which was built to resist the threat of invasion by Napoleon, three regular battalions staged a tattoo outlining the regiment's history. Afterwards the Queen met junior ranks and their families.

December 1975: The Queen visited the Royal British Legion Village at Preston Hall, Aylesford, as part of its Golden Jubilee celebrations. She visited the poppy factory, fancy goods warehouse and the signs department, chatting to officials and workers. Hundreds of schoolchildren in Aylesford were given the afternoon off so they could see the royal visitor.

October 1976: The Duke of Edinburgh had a lesson in rope making when he opened the Merchant Navy College in Greenhithe. The Duke, a former Royal Navy officer, clearly enjoyed the nautical flavour of the £3.2 million complex which was designed to resemble a large cargo ship.

December 1978: Visiting Australians Brandon and Damien Wood held up their country's flag to welcome the Duchess of Kent to Templer Barracks, Ashford, where their father was on an exchange visit. The Duchess, Controller Commandant of the Women's Royal Army Corps, was shown the role played by the WRAC in the Intelligence Corps.

October 1979: Princess Anne enjoyed her visit to the Intelligence Corps at Templer Barracks, Ashford. Lt-Colonel Mark Durman introduced her to some of the servicemen's families.

May 1980: Charles Busby, chairman of the Royal British Legion Industries, led three cheers for the Duchess of Kent after she officially opened Charles Busby Court, a block of flats named after him at the Royal British Legion Village, Preston Hall, Aylesford, near Maidstone.

June 1980: These Royal Marines bandsmen made Princess Anne smile when she visited HMS *Pembroke* at Chatham as Chief Commandant of the Women's Royal Naval Service. She had a word with every one of the 104 Wrens at the base.

June 1980: The 40th anniversary of Dunkirk was marked by a ceremony in Ramsgate at which the Queen Mother was guest of honour. She took part in a memorial service and received the salute as the band of the Royal Corps of Transport led the veterans in a march past. Many of the veterans were able to speak to the Queen Mother afterwards. Some showed her their prized photographs taken when she reviewed them with her late husband, King George VI, before they sailed for France with the British Expeditionary Force in 1939.

December 1983: Children from the Royal British Legion Playgroup at Aylesford, waved goodbye to the Duchess of Kent's helicopter after she arrived to open the Legion's Churchill Centre, a rehabilitation and assessment unit.

March 1981: These youngsters came ready with Union Jacks when the Queen visited the Intelligence Corps at Templer Barracks, Ashford.

March 1985: The Royal Engineers had plenty of surprises in store for Prince Charles when he visited them at Chattenden Barracks, Gillingham. They let him get behind the wheel of this giant army vehicle and invited him to crush a Jaguar that looked exactly like his own car. In fact it was a wreck from a scrapheap that the Sappers had spruced up.

The Prince came face to face with this German bomb, nicknamed Hermann, which the Chattenden bomb squad had recently defused in Sheffield.

June 1986: Standard bearers formed a magnificent guard of honour for the Duchess of Kent at the entrance to the Mountbatten Pavilion at the Royal British Legion Village, Aylesford. She officially opened the hostel for single disabled ex-servicemen who work for British Legion Industries or are receiving treatment at the village's Churchill Rehabilitation Centre. It was the Duchess's fourth visit since 1969 to the village of which she is patron.

May 1987: It was all smiles when the Queen visited the Royal Engineers at Brompton Barracks, Gillingham, to celebrate the bicentenary of the regiment's royal title. She also officially opened the Royal Engineers' museum in the Ravelin Building. The Queen toured exhibitions of the Sappers' work and saw bomb disposal experts in action. She even blew up a bridge after signing an authorisation as Colonel-in-Chief, permitting herself to do so.

July 1989: The Queen Mother paid tribute to the Normandy Veterans when she unveiled a plaque to them during a simple service in Canterbury Cathedral. Afterwards she made her way to Cathedral House where she met 12 of the veterans in the Chapter House. She then she went outside to take the salute of a march past of hundreds of Normandy veterans from all over the country.

June 1993: The Princess of Wales was an instant hit with the officers and men of her namesake regiment when she paid her first visit to Howe Barracks, Canterbury. She inspected the regular and territorial battalions of the newly-formed Princess of Wales's Royal Regiment which had been created by the amalgamation of the Queen's and Royal Hampshires. She spoke of her pride at standing before the regiment as its Colonel-in-Chief and joked: "It has to be said that for a 31-year-old woman to have 2,500 men under her command is quite a feat."

September 1993: As patron and Commander-in-Chief of the Royal Naval Auxiliary Service, Prince Michael made his first and last visit to the Chatham unit the year before the service was disbanded. He was saying farewell to the Thames group of the RNXS which included Chatham, Sheerness and Gravesend and units in the London area. He took part in exercises on the River Medway before meeting the auxiliaries on HMS *Wildfire*.

February 1994: The Queen came to Folkestone to celebrate the 200th anniversary of the Argyll and Sutherland Highlanders Regiment of which she is Colonel-in-Chief. She visited the 650 soldiers at Shorncliffe Barracks where they had been based for the past year. The Queen attended a service at St Mark's garrison church then, after lunch, watched a scuba diving demonstration, unveiled a picture of the regiment, signed a scroll and started a sponsored cycle ride by eight soldiers to Stirling. She is pictured enjoying a laugh with one of the cyclists.

June 1995: The Queen was full of smiles when she visited the Royal Green Jackets at the Lydd Army Training Centre. The Queen, Colonel-in-Chief of the regiment, spent three hours at the centre, watching firing exercises, seeing photographs of the soldiers on overseas exercises and enjoying lunch with the officers, men and their families.

May 1995: Princess Diana presented her regiment, the Princess of Wales's Royal Regiment, with its new colours at Howe Barracks, Canterbury. The band struck up the tune *Hey Look Me Over* as the Colonel-in-Chief walked across the parade ground – and she did just that, strolling among the ranks, stopping frequently to talk. She presented the new standards to Lieutenant Adam Crawley and Second Lieutenant Adam Rout. Until then the regiment had marched behind the colours of the Queen's and the Royal Hampshires, the two regiments from which it was formed.

EDUCATION AND YOUNG PEOPLE

ROYAL visits half a century or more ago tended to be very formal affairs. They were probably more frightening than enjoyable for most people who would have been over-awed at the prospect of speaking to a member of the royal family.

But the Duchess of York, as the Queen Mother then was, showed she already had the common touch in 1933 when she spent a happy hour and a half with pupils during a visit to the Caldecott Community School in Maidstone.

It is a trend that has continued through many royal visits to Kent's schools, colleges, youth clubs and sports centres.

Sixty years later, Princess Diana, was able to sit down and play snap with children at a Barnados day care centre in Tunbridge Wells, and even to cuddle youngsters on her knee.

Most royal visits are not as informal as that, but certainly thousands of young people in Kent have enjoyed the chance to show off their skills and talk about their school work, their sport and their hobbies to members of the royal family.

And since 1955 many students in Kent have been able to boast that their university had a royal chancellor.

That year the Queen Mother became chancellor of the University of London, of which Wye College near Ashford is a part. She attended formal commemoration ceremonies there and also mingled with guests at a garden party afterwards.

Her granddaughter, Princess Anne, took over as London University chancellor in 1981 and she too has visited Wye College.

The University of Kent, which opened in 1966, had Princess Marina, Duchess of Kent, as its first chancellor.

July 1993: The Duchess of York, now the Queen Mother, visited Caldecott Community School, Mote House, Maidstone, where she spent a happy, relaxed time with the children. Pupils presented her with a hand-woven bag as a memento of her visit. The school, which had opened in Maidstone the previous September, had 67 pupils from homes where conditions were 'in any way abnormal, unhappy or undesirable'.

The Duchess is seen here with Lord Lytton, vice-president of the community, and Miss L.M.Rendel, lady superintendent of the school.

June 1936: The Duke of Kent, patron of Kent Council of Social Services, made a whirlwind tour of North West and West Kent. He dropped in at Mayplace Road Junior School, in Crayford, to see the operation of a scheme under which children were provided with milk. But the royal visit seemed to overwhelm five-year-old Sheila Ward, who was reluctant to accept her bottle from the Duke.

VISIT TO KENT

Toys For Children
At
Training School

JOYOUS SCENES

QUEEN MARY brought gifts of toys for the children when she paid an informal visit to the Margaret McMillan Nursery School at Wrotham, on Monday afternoon.

Arriving at 3.15, Queen Mary was welcomed by Lady Astor, Governor of the Rachael McMillan Training School, with which the school at Wrotham is connected.

Queen Mary was conducted round the school by Lady Astor. She displayed great interest in the activities there and talked with the children.

After tea Queen Mary was photographed with the children. Her Majesty left at 5.15.

Queen Mary, who was well acquainted with Margaret Mc...

July 1937: Queen Mary brought gifts of toys for the children when she visited the Margaret McMillan Nursery School at Wrotham. She was shown round by Lady Astor, governor of the Rachael McMillan Training School, with which the Wrotham school was associated. This illustration was taken from a page in the *Kent Messenger*.

1948: The Queen visited the Caldecott Community at Mersham-le-Hatch, near Ashford, where she chatted with pupils as she was shown round by the headmistress, Miss L.M.Rendel.

May 1950: Princess Margaret was in Canterbury to help St Edmund's School celebrate its bicentenary. Her father, King George VI, was its patron. She is seen presenting Latin, Greek, English and Natural History prizes to J.M.Taylor.

July 1951: Huge crowds of holidaymakers greeted Princess Elizabeth as she was driven along the seafront at Margate on her way to the Royal School for Deaf and Dumb Children in the town. She had travelled from London in the Pullman coach of a special train chartered by the school for 400 parents and friends. The Princess was the first member of the royal family to visit the school since the Prince of Wales in 1925. A marquee was set up in the grounds to display pupils' needlework, tailoring, carpentry and other skills. To demonstrate the high standard of their work, they presented the Princess with a dress they had made for her 11-month-old baby daughter, Anne. About 1,200 guests assembled on the sports field for the prize-giving ceremony. Here the Princess is seen being introduced to members of the school's committee by its treasurer, Lord Ebury.

October 1953: These rugby players met the Queen Mother when she visited Tonbridge School and opened a memorial gateway to mark its 400th anniversary. She toured the school and saw everything from rehearsals of the school play (*Henry IV, Part I*) to the rugby match. Earlier in the day she had become the first royal visitor to Marden Fruit Show.

March 1956: The Queen Mother visited Cranbrook School for the celebrations to mark 25 years of service by headmaster Russell Scott. She was taken on a tour of the school and met prefects and Old Boys, among them broadcaster Peter West, secretary of the Old Cranbrookians' Association.

May 1957: Princess Alexandra spent two hours at Dartford College of Physical Education to open a £27,000 gymnasium. The Princess, who had earlier lunched with the Mayor and Corporation of Dartford, told students, staff and guests that her great-grandmother, Queen Alexandra, had witnessed a demonstration arranged by the college founder, Madame Ostenberg, a year before it opened. She also recalled that her grandparents, King George V and Queen Mary had visited the college during World War One.

November 1958: Jane Nye, a student of Wye College, near Ashford, explained to the Duke of Edinburgh an experiment she was conducting.

July 1962: The Queen Mother passed between the ranks of scholars on her way to the Great Hall at the King's School, Canterbury, where she unveiled a plaque to Canon Frederick Shirley, who was retiring after 27 years as headmaster.

November 1962: Princess Alexandra opened the South Wing, Smythe Library and Ironside Cloister at Tonbridge School, just a few days before the official announcement of her engagement to the Hon Angus Ogilvy. She toured the school and visited the art school and workshops opened by her father, the late Duke of Kent, in 1936. Here she admires a harpsichord being built by pupils.

July 1965: The Queen Mother was guest of honour at a garden party at Withersdane Hall, Wye College, in her role as Chancellor of the University of London. She mingled with the 1,000 guests and delighted many of them by stopping for a chat.

Earlier in the day, the Queen Mother attended the college's annual commemoration ceremony. She is seen here wearing the red robes of a Doctor of Literature as she walked to Wye Church for the commemoration service.

March 1966: Princess Marina, Duchess of Kent, was installed as the first Chancellor of the new University of Kent at Canterbury and also became its first graduate. She was admitted to an honorary doctorate by the Pro-Chancellor, Lord Cornwallis, and the Vice-Chancellor, Dr Geoffrey Templeman. Canterbury Cathedral bells pealed a welcome for the Duchess when she attended a service there to mark the foundation of the university.

December 1966: Princess Margaret paid her first visit to Ashford – in pouring rain. She opened the St John Ambulance Brigade Ashford Corps in Barrow Hill then drove to Ashford School to open its new assembly block, the Lilian Brake building, named after one of the school's founders. Here she is pictured in a chemistry laboratory.

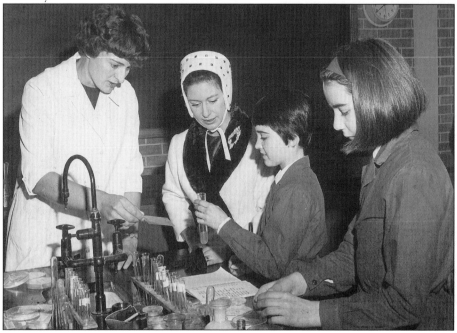

May 1967: Messing about with paint has always been popular with children and this little one was not going to let a royal visitor get in the way. Princess Margaret was paying a return visit to St Christopher's Nursery Training College at Tunbridge Wells as president of Dr Barnado's. She had first been to the college in 1948, a year after it was bought for Dr Barnado's as a training centre for nurses. She met children's entertainer Mr Pastry (Richard Hearne, of Maidstone) who handed over a cheque for £500 and an anonymous gift of £100 towards the swimming pool his fund was providing at the Princess Margaret School, Taunton, Devon. The Princess flew from Tunbridge Wells to Canterbury to visit the new Dr Barnado's home, Woodlands, at St Thomas's Hill, overlooking the city.

November 1967: The Duchess of Kent joined in the singing at the official opening of the YMCA and Church Institute Y Sports Centre in Maidstone.

May 1968: Faversham had its first royal visitor for 30 years when Princess Alexandra opened the £300,000 Queen Elizabeth School, a co-educational grammar created by the amalgamation of the Williams Gibbs School for girls and Faversham Grammar for boys. Her tour of the school included an inspection of the sports facilities where she met these tennis players.

March 1968: Princess Marina, the Duchess of Kent, chatted to students after unveiling a plaque to mark the official opening of Sittingbourne College of Education.

March 1968: The Duke of Edinburgh found something to amuse him when he visited this workshop at Hadlow College, near Tonbridge.

1969: Students on the dry ski slope shared a joke with the Duke of Edinburgh when he officially opened the Bowles Outdoor Pursuits Centre at Eridge, near Tunbridge Wells. He also saw police cadets, schoolchildren and youth hostel groups from all over the south-east learning rock-climbing, canoeing and camping techniques.

May 1970: Princess Anne returned to her old school, Benenden, to open a £62,500 sixth-form block and staff room. It was her first official visit since she left school in 1968. She is seen here with her old headmistress, Elizabeth Clarke.

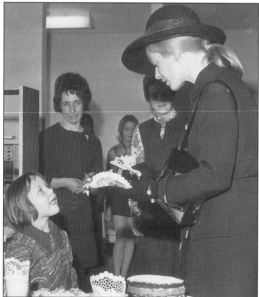

March 1971: The Duchess of Kent unveiled a commemorative lectern to mark the official opening of Sheppey School. She then toured classrooms chatting to pupils and staff, and met two-to four-year-olds in the childcare section of the domestic economy department. Here she is seen with four-year-old Dawn Baker.

November 1971: The Duchess of Kent went to the Odeon Cinema in Ashford not to see *M.A.S.H* but to attend Ashford School's prize-giving there. She later opened a new dining room at the school.

August 1972: Amanda Barham, eight, presented Princess Anne with a posy at Folkestone Roller Dance Club. The Princess unveiled a plaque.

May 1974: Cranbrook School head boy David Hall chatted to the Duchess of Kent when she opened a £150,000 sixth-form centre as part of the school's 400th anniversary celebrations.

November 1974: These donkeys caught the attention of Princess Anne when she visited Fairfield House School for deprived girls, in Broadstairs, run by the Bromley and Beckenham branch of the Save the Children Fund. She unveiled a plaque in the new gym at the school. She is seen here with headmistress Adrienne Brooke.

July 1975: A moment of family sporting history was recalled for the Duchess of Kent when she opened St Mary's Hall at the King's School, Canterbury. Colin Fairservice, master in charge of games, told her he caught her father, Sir William Worsley, out during a cricket match against Yorkshire in 1929.

April 1976: The Queen Mother visited the Royal School for the Deaf at Margate to open its £1 million new buildings.

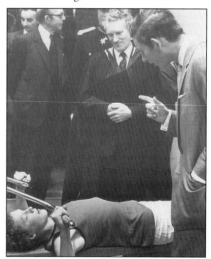

April 1977: The Prince of Wales opened the £500,000 Marley Sports Centre at Sevenoaks School. It was presented to the school by the Marley Tile Company which was celebrating its 50th anniversary. The Prince had a few words of advice for Michael Robinson, 16, who was demonstrating equipment in the gym.

July 1980: The Prince of Wales helped Norton Knatchbull School, Ashford, celebrate its 350th anniversary by opening its new sports pavilion. As he toured the school his attention was caught by this work by student Graham Smith.

November 1980: Princess Alice tried her hand at the ancient Kentish game of bat and trap when she opened the Civil Service Sports Association Club in Watling Street, Gillingham. She also saw demonstrations of football, karate and bowls.

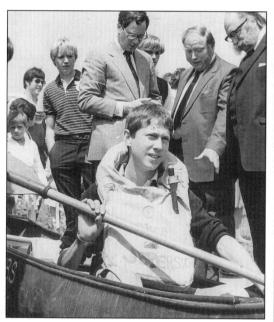

June 1983: The Duke of Gloucester, president of the National Association of Boys' Clubs, dropped in at the Space Boys' Club, Lilac Road, Strood, as part of a tour of clubs in North Kent. Club chairman John Persich and president Ticker Fry showed him round the club and talked to him about its members' next challenge, a 100 mile canoe trip down the River Rhine.

July 1984: Princess Anne carried out her first duties at Wye College after taking over from the Queen Mother as Chancellor of the University of London. She wore the black and gold robes previously worn by her grandmother during her years as Chancellor. The Princess attended a commemoration service in the village church in the morning and the commemoration ceremony in Withersdane Hall in the afternoon. The Provost, Reg Older, welcomed her in front of 1,000 guests.

November 1985: Matthew Crocker, 10, was busy making mince pies for tea when the Queen Mother opened the Caldecott Community Home, Lacton House, at Willesborough, Ashford.

March 1988: Keith Philips received some encouraging words from the Duchess of Kent when she visited Valence School for the handicapped at Westerham, near Sevenoaks. She and the Duke of Kent planted trees at the school as part of a tour of the Sevenoaks area for the trust fund, Trees for the Future, which raised money to repair woodland damaged by the 1987 hurricane.

June 1988: Lewis Wibley, five, presented a posy to Princess Michael of Kent when she arrived for the official opening of Kingfisher School, Princes Park, Chatham. On that day she also visited the first Child Safety Day at Chatham Historic Dockyard.

March 1990: The Princess of Wales gave this little girl a cuddle during a visit to Barnados Ravensdale Day Care Centre in Tunbridge Wells which caters for under-fives with special needs. The Princess, president of Barnardos, also visited the charity's Chilston Mediation and Family Service Project in the town.

May 1992: Prince Edward shared a laugh with these young people at the Artwise Factory, part of Ramsgate Youth Centre in St Luke's Avenue. The Metamorphosis Youth Theatre Company entertained him with sketches and poetry. He also opened a ferry terminal at Ramsgate.

SHOWS, PAGEANTS, BALLS & FÊTES

THERE was great excitement when it became known that the Prince of Wales was to open the Kent County Fair in Mote Park, Maidstone, in June 1934. In those pre-television days the royal family seemed much more remote and chances to see them at close quarters were fairly rare.

When the Prince arrived in the arena he was welcomed by 5,000 children – Boy Scouts, Girl Guides and boys from the training ship, *Arethusa*.

The girls spelled out a welcome to the Prince with their flags: 'The youth of Kent offer their loyal greetings.'

They might not spell out the message in quite the same way today, but even now, more than 60 years later, people will flock to see a royal visitor to Kent County Agricultural Show, the Ashford Fat Stock Show or Marden Fruit Show.

They crowd round, trying to get take photos, or, better still, snatch a word with the royal guest.

The County Show, in particular, has enjoyed a fair number of royal visitors – including the Queen, who opened the Diamond Jubilee show in 1989, and Princess Alexandra who opened the new county show ground at Detling, near Maidstone, in 1964.

But the big shows are not the only opportunity for people to see the royal family at close quarters in a fairly relaxed atmosphere.

Princess Anne, Princess Margaret, the Duke and Duchess of Gloucester and The Duke and Duchess of Kent have all attended public or semi-public functions, such as balls, fashion shows and fêtes in Kent to help the charities with which they are involved.

And both the Duke of Edinburgh and his son, Prince Edward, have joined in the fun at events to celebrate the Duke of Edinburgh Award Schemes.

July 1926: Princess Mary, president of the Girl Guides Association, inspected 7,000 Girl Guides and Brownies at Gillingham Park. The girls, from all over the county, gave a number of displays and demonstrated their signalling and first aid skills.

June 1934: Prince of Wales opened the Kent County Fair at Mote Park, Maidstone. He flew into Rochester Airport then drove to Maidstone with the Lord Lieutenant of Kent, Lord Camden. The royal visitor was shown around the show by Major J.S.Hatfeild, chairman of the Kent Community Council which organised the fair. Here they are seen watching an anti-gas defence demonstration.

The Daily Sketch Life Line was one of the attractions of the show.

June 1935: The following year it was the turn of the Prince of Wales's brother, Prince George, Duke of Kent, to open the County Fair, again at Mote Park, Maidstone. He is pictured talking to this officer of the Girls' Life Brigade.

The Prince left Mote Park in this open-topped car.

July 1935: A month later the Duke of Kent was back at another show, this time the Kent County Agricultural Show in Ashford. Little Eleanor Bacon, daughter of the Kent Agricultural Society Show secretary, Major Bacon, was unimpressed both by the basket of cherries by her side and by the royal visitor.

July 1936: The Duke of Kent was guest of honour at the Tunbridge Wells Agricultural Show the following year. This time he was accompanied by his wife who was already a firm favourite with the people of Kent.

July 1939: The clouds of war were looming dark ahead when the Duke of Kent visited the Kent County Agricultural Show in Folkestone. He is seen inspecting prize-winning cattle.

July 1946: Somerset de Chair, the owner of Chilham Castle, was happy to welcome the Duchess of Kent to the opening performance of his pageant which told the history of England from a Chilham perspective. He wrote the pageant himself and played the part of the ostler. Sir Edward Hardy, chairman of Kent County Council, played Sir Dudley Digger, who built the Jacobean mansion and adjoining castle keep in 1616; Major Leslie Chalk of Tenterden played King Henry VIII and Mrs B.Sconce took the role of Anne Boleyn. About 4,000 people watched the pageant unfold.

July 1958: Princess Alexandra was impressed by the work of this spinner at Kent County Agricultural Show.

July 1961: Princess Alexandra joined in the Kent celebrations of the Golden Jubilee of the National Association of Mixed Clubs and Girls' Clubs. About 1,000 people attended the event at Hunton Court, Hunton, home of Mr and Mrs G.C.Devas. Among the young people demonstrating the huge range of activities carried out in clubs across the county were The Whirlwinds, a rock group from St Nicholas Youth Fellowship in Maidstone. The line up was: Michael Stephens on drums, Colin Honey, bass guitar, Joe Bailey on vocals, Dave Carter, rhythm guitar, Chuck J.Ford on lead guitar and Andy Cheeseman on vocals. Princess Alexandra told them how much she had enjoyed their rendition of *Summer Time* and *Running Bear*.

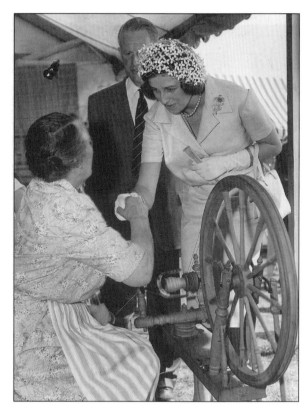

July 1962: The Tunbridge Wells Agricultural Show celebrated its centenary with a visit by the Queen Mother, who is seen admiring the Champion Dairy Female after presenting the prizes. She had paid her first visit to the Tunbridge Wells show 30 years earlier.

December 1968: The Duke of Edinburgh visited the 100th Ashford Fat Stock Show with its president, Lord Brabourne.

July 1969: Lord Cornwallis, Lord Lieutenant of Kent, swept the Duchess of Kent on to the dance floor for the first dance of the evening at a charity ball which raised about £700 for the Kent Association of Boys' Clubs. About 500 guests attended the ball, at St Clere, Kemsing, home of Brigadier and Mrs Hugh Norman.

May 1972: The Duke and Duchess of Kent were keen to take part in the prize draw at the Kent County Playing Fields Association Ball at Brompton Barracks, Gillingham. The event marked the end of the association's appeal year, during which it raised £30,000.

May 1971: This young cyclist had a chat with the Duchess of Kent at a garden party at the home of Stanley Blow, in Matfield, near Tonbridge. It raised about £1,000 for the Kent County Playing Fields Association, of which the Duchess is patron.

July 1972: Princess Anne became the first member of the royal family to compete in the Kent County Show. She took third place in the Spillers Open Competition.

July 1973: Princess Alexandra visited the *Kent Messenger* stand at the County Show.

October 1977: Princess Margaret, president of Dr Barnado's, was among the guests at the charity's Silver Jubilee Ball at Linton Park, Maidstone. It raised £2,500 of the £5,000 needed for the Dr Barnado's Kenward Home in Heathfield Road, Maidstone. She is seen here at dinner sharing a joke with Lord Astor of Hever and John Hillyer, treasurer of Dr Barnardo's.

June 1979: Princess Margaret was guest of honour at a fashion show at Leeds Castle in aid of one of her favourite charities, The Dockland Settlement Trust.

July 1979: The Golden Jubilee Kent County Agricultural Show was opened by the Duke of Gloucester. The Duke, wearing a snappy Panama hat, took a professional interest in the stands and livestock as head of his family's 2,000 acre estate.

October 1979: Prince and Princess Michael of Kent were guests at a party to launch a three-day flower festival at Leeds Castle. The Princess is seen chatting to Lord Cornwallis.

June 1981: Pouring rain could not dampen the enthusiasm of 7,000 youngsters who gathered at Hever Castle to celebrate the 25th anniversary of the Duke of Edinburgh Award scheme with the help of the Duke himself. They took part in an *It's a Knockout* contest and had fun at the many side shows and stalls.

July 1982: Youngsters from the Pestalozzi children's village in Sedlescombe, East Sussex, dressed in national costume and danced on the lawns of Leeds Castle, near Maidstone, to greet the Duke and Duchess of Gloucester. Afterwards the youngsters had the chance to speak to the Duchess. She and her husband were guests of honour at a charity concert in aid of the village.

October 1983: This giant apple took the fancy of the Duke of Gloucester at Marden Fruit Show.

July 1984: Princess Anne and the Lord Lieutenant of Kent, Robin Leigh-Pemberton, travelled in style in this carriage drawn by two Whitbread shire dray horses. The Princess was at Leeds Castle, near Maidstone, as president of the Save the Children Fund to attend a fête organised by its Kent branch.

July 1989: What better way could be found to celebrate the Diamond Jubilee of the Kent County Agricultural Show than with a visit by the Queen and Prince Philip? The Queen cut the ribbon to open the showground's new £150,000 pavilion then joined the other 21,000 visitors looking round the show. She made history when she entered the soft fruit tent. Every year the show's finest cherries have been sent to Buckingham Palace for the Queen to enjoy. This year she received them personally from the soft fruit show chairman's wife, Phyllis Worley, who presented them on behalf of the grower, Faversham farmer Basil Neame.

July 1994: the Duchess of Kent enjoyed tasting the cherries at the County Show.

June 1995: Princess Alexandra joined the National Trust's centenary celebrations by attending a garden party at the Trust-owned Scotney Castle at Lamberhurst. She brought with her a tulip tree donated by the National Trust's president, the Queen Mother, which she planted in the grounds to replace one blown down by high winds.

KENT'S CATHEDRALS

KING George VI's visit to Canterbury Cathedral in July 1946 marked a new era of royal interest in the city's ancient cathedral, the seat of Christianity in Britain. He arrived with the Queen and their daughter, Princess Elizabeth, for a service of thanksgiving for the preservation of the cathedral from the ravages of war.

And in so doing he became the first reigning monarch to set foot in it since King Charles II in 1660.

He also signalled his support by becoming a member of the Friends of Canterbury Cathedral.

It is a support from the royal family which has lasted through the years and which has also extended to Rochester Cathedral.

The present Queen, who attended Royal Maundy Services in Rochester in 1961 and Canterbury in 1965, spent an enjoyable day in Canterbury in 1976, taking a close interest in the restoration work.

Prince Charles, too, whose interest in architecture is well known, showed his concern for Canterbury Cathedral by agreeing to become President of the Trustees of the Restoration Appeal.

Princess Marina, Duchess of Kent, was patron of the Friends of Rochester Cathedral, a role which the present Duchess of Kent was proud to take on after the death of her mother-in-law.

Most importantly, the royal family has been involved in almost every major event taking place in the cathedrals – enthronements of the Archbishops, the 800th anniversary of the Martyrdom of Thomas Becket and, more recently, the celebrations to mark the 1,400th anniversary of the arrival of St Augustine in England.

July 1946: Thousands of well-wishers gathered in Canterbury to see the King, Queen and Princess Elizabeth arrive for a service of thanksgiving for the preservation of the cathedral through the war. The royal family toured the ancient city and saw the Roman tessellated pavement uncovered by bombing. The King became the first reigning monarch to visit the King's School since Queen Elizabeth I in the 16th century who had a Latin oration read to her by the Queen's Scholar. King George presented a Royal Charter to the Dean, Dr Hewlett Johnson, chairman of the governors of this, the oldest school in the country.

August 1947: Princess Elizabeth was back at the King's School the following year to attend a conference of the Church of England Youth Council of which she had recently become the president. The event attracted delegates from 30 dioceses in England, from 10 national youth organisations and from overseas, including the USA and China. It was followed by a short service in the cathedral.

August 1949: Princess Elizabeth and Prince Philip attended a service at Canterbury Cathedral to mark Kent's part in the celebrations of the Silver Jubilee of the National Playing Fields Association of which the Prince is president. The Archbishop of Canterbury, Dr Geoffrey Fisher, preached the sermon.

March 1961: Huge crowds turned out to welcome the Queen and Prince Philip to Rochester for the Maundy Service in the cathedral. The couple walked from the Guildhall along the High Street to the

cathedral for the distribution of the Maundy money. Here, the Queen and Prince chatted to clergy outside the West Door of the cathedral.

April 1965: This year the Queen distributed Maundy money at Canterbury Cathedral. She and Prince Philip flew into Manston then drove to Canterbury where they were greeted by trumpeters from the Queen's Own Buffs, The Royal Kent Regiment. They are seen here with the Dean of Canterbury, the Very Rev Ian White-Thomson, receiving posies from Michael Strutt, Lucy White-Thomson, Andrew Newell and Lavina Wicks.

April 1966: Princess Margaret opened a £60,000 extension to Graham Chiesman House, the Rochester Diocesan Youth Conference and Retreat House, at Chislehurst. She travelled from Bromley where she had presented a £1,200 specially equipped bus from the town's young people to the aged and disabled. She was accompanied on her tour of Graham Chiesman House by the Bishop of Rochester, the Rt Rev Richard Say. She also met Kent and England cricketer Colin Cowdrey, chairman of the Diocesan Youth Council. His father-in-law, Stuart Chiesman, gave the house, his former home, to the diocese in memory of his son, Graham, who was killed in an accident as a young boy. The Princess is seen here with Susan Nutter of Petts Wood, Carol Drew of Beckenham, and Joan Quaife of Rochester.

June 1968: Princess Marina made four visits in Rochester. She toured King's School, made an official call at the Guildhall, visited the French Hospital, La Providence, which was celebrating its 250th anniversary, then attended the Festival Service of the Friends of Rochester Cathedral, of which she was patron.

July 1970: The Archbishop of Canterbury, Dr Michael Ramsey led the Queen Mother into Canterbury Cathedral for a service to mark the 800th anniversary of the Martyrdom of Thomas Becket. It was attended by prelates from all over the world.

July 1971: These nursing cadets from the Medway Towns and Dartford met Princess Alexandra during Kent Red Cross Society's parade and service of thanksgiving at Canterbury Cathedral.

January 1975: Dr Donald Coggan became the 101st Archbishop of Canterbury, taking over from Dr Michael Ramsey. Prince Charles, Princess Margaret and the Duchess of Kent represented the Monarchy at his enthronement in Canterbury Cathedral. The Lord Lieutenant of Kent, Lord Astor of Hever, and Lady Astor accompanied the royal party.

December 1976: The Queen spent five hours at Canterbury Cathedral inspecting the restoration work being carried out there. Her visit coincided with the announcement that the restoration fund had reached £2.5 million. The Queen showed a keen interest in the work of the glaziers and masons. Stained glass expert Frederick Cole told her that the priceless 12th and 13th century glass had been in danger from atmospheric acids before the restoration work was carried out.

March 1980: Robert Runcie was enthroned as the 102nd Archbishop of Canterbury in front of a congregation of 3,000 men and women from all over the world. Princess Margaret, with her nephew Prince Charles at her side, smiled and clapped enthusiastically as the congregation broke into applause in a spontaneous gesture of affection for the new Archbishop. They are seen here arriving at the cathedral.

March 1980: Prince Charles visited Canterbury Cathedral as president of the Trustees of the Cathedral Appeal. He is seen talking to Kent Archaeological Trust member John Rady about the work it was carrying out at the cathedral.

June 1986: The Duchess of Kent, who, like her mother-in-law before her, agreed to be patron of the Friends of Rochester Cathedral, paid her first visit there to attend a thanksgiving service to celebrate the Friends' 50th anniversary.

December 1986: An advent carol service at Canterbury Cathedral for more than 1,100 children turned into a royal celebration when Princess Diana decided to attend. She made the day special for the hundreds of people who had turned out to see her on a cold December day, by smiling, waving and talking to as many of them as possible. Here she is seen leaving the cathedral with the Archbishop, Dr Robert Runcie.

March 1987: The Queen smiled happily at the crowds in Canterbury when she was in the city to open Cathedral House, the administrative hub of the cathedral. She and the Duke of Edinburgh inspected restoration work in the Crypt and attended Choral Evensong. The Queen also opened the Poor Priests' Hospital heritage centre and a computing laboratory at the University of Kent.

April 1991: Princess Diana and Princess Margaret were among the crowds who braved wind and rain to attend the enthronement of Dr George Carey as Archbishop of Canterbury. They landed in a red helicopter of the Queen's Flight at the Victoria Recreation Ground where they were greeted by the Lord Lieutenant of Kent, Robin Leigh-Pemberton. But the wind showed scant regard for royalty. A gust snatched Princess Diana's wide-brimmed hat off her head, sending it rolling away on its brim. A gallant equerry rescued it for her. The Princess is seen making sure her hat stays put.

May 1997: More than 2,000 people from all over the world packed into Canterbury Cathedral to celebrate the 1,400th anniversary of the arrival of St Augustine in England. The congregation, which included Prince Charles, witnessed the procession of the sixth-century Italian gospel thought to have been brought to England by St Augustine in 597. The Latin version of the Bible, known as the Canterbury Gospels, is in the possession of Corpus Christi College, Cambridge, and is normally only brought to Canterbury for the enthronement of Archbishops. Prince Charles arrived at the cathedral accompanied by the Dean, the Very Rev Dr John Simpson. The service, conducted by the Archbishop, Dr George Carey, was attended by the Archbishop of Westminster, Cardinal Basil Hume, Archbishop Barbarito, representing the Pope, and former Archbishops of Canterbury Lord Runcie and Lord Coggan.

THE LORD WARDEN OF THE CINQUE PORTS

THE Queen Mother both upheld centuries of tradition and broke with tradition when she became Lord Warden of the Cinque Ports in 1979. She was the first woman to hold the ancient office which has been combined with that of Constable of Dover Castle since 1226. The Lord Warden of the Cinque Ports – Hasting, Romney, Hythe, Dover, and Sandwich – and the Two Ancient Towns – Rye and Winchelsea – was charged with the crucial job of controlling the Channel ports which were vital to the Navy and to trade. It was an office that carried great power and prestige.

But today's Lord Warden has a purely ceremonial role, one that delights the people of East Kent who have been happy to welcome the Queen Mother for her annual visits to her official residence in Walmer Castle.

She described her installation in July 1979 as the happiest day of her life.

It was a day of great pomp and pageantry, of course, but for the thousands of spectators it was the Queen Mother's friendliness and informality that made it so special.

She has continued to charm the people of the Cinque Ports and beyond. She has not stood on ceremony, locked away in Walmer Castle. Instead she has been out and about meeting people – attending church, visiting schools, clubs, enjoying her garden, getting to know the area.

She even championed the cause of Folkestone in 1993 when she wrote to the Department of Transport expressing her concern at plans to remove the town's name from road signs in favour of Eurotunnel.

No wonder this Lord Warden has become such a favourite with the people of East Kent.

July 1979: The Queen Mother arrived at Dover from Greenwich aboard the Royal Yacht *Britannia* for her installation as Lord Warden. A Force Six wind meant *Britannia* could not dock so the royal party was ferried ashore by launch. Here the Queen Mother is welcomed to Dover by Lord Astor of Hever, Lord Lieutenant of Kent.

Princess Margaret's son Lord Linley, 17, arriving at Constable's Tower, Dover Castle, before the ceremony.

His sister, Lady Sarah Armstrong Jones, 15.

Prince Edward, 15, acted as his grandmother's escort as they toured Dover Castle.

The Queen Mother travelled down from Dover Castle by carriage.

The new Lord Warden stopped to chat to some of the thousands of people who lined the streets of Dover.

She inspected a Guard of Honour.

It may have been a day of pomp and circumstance but the Queen Mother could not resist the chance to talk to Jonathan Buckhurst, of Bridge, near Canterbury, about his 13-week-old miniature Dachshund, Tigga.

A spectacular air display above *Britannia*.

July 1980: Just a year after her installation as Lord Warden and the Queen Mother was already getting to know her new domain better. She dropped into New Romney where she met councillors and Town Hall staff in the council chamber. The excitement was too much for Brownie Juliette Payne, nine, who stepped out of the crowd to offer a pink rose to the royal visitor, then just burst into tears. But the Queen Mother came to the rescue by reaching out sympathetically to wipe away the tears and asking kindly: "Did you pick it in your own garden?"

June 1982: The Kent and East Sussex Railway at Tenterden welcomed its first royal passenger when the Queen Mother travelled in a new carriage named *Diana* after her eldest grandson's wife.

She also saw a specially adapted carriage for disabled people making its maiden trip. On board was Peter Sinclair, 12, of Bearsted, pictured here, a muscular dystrophy sufferer whose parents had converted the carriage.

July 1989: The Queen Mother sailed into Dover on board the Royal Yacht *Britannia* again to celebrate 10 years as Lord Warden of the Cinque Ports. She went to a thanksgiving service, visited St Mary's Primary School in Dover and attended a special meeting of the Court of Brotherhood and Eastling at Dover Town Hall. In the evening she received guests on board *Britannia* and watched the Royal Marines beat retreat on the Prince of Wales Pier.

July 1992: Pupils and staff celebrated the 200th anniversary of the Royal School for Deaf Children in Margate with a visit from its patron, the Queen Mother. It was her second visit to the school which was the first public institution for deaf children in the country. She opened new school buildings in 1976.

July 1991: The Lord Warden met these young gymnasts in the sports hall of Sandwich Sports and Leisure Centre. She opened the centre during a hectic weekend in Kent which included morning service at St Mary's, Walmer, the opening of the parish house, Elizabeth House, lunch with the Deputy Constable of Dover Castle, Brigadier John Holman, and a visit to the White Cliffs Experience, Dover – all on the first day.

July 1994: The Queen Mother amazed onlookers and organisers alike in Lydd when she decided not to get into the car laid on to take her from The Rype, where her helicopter had landed, to the community hall. Instead she walked there, stopping to talk to many in the waiting crowds along the way. After opening the hall she met some of the people who would use it: majorettes, the drama group, the karate club and the tennis club.

July 1995: Nicola Clark, 10, presented the Queen Mother with a posy when she visited Sunny Corner sheltered housing scheme for the elderly at Aycliffe, Dover.

FAMILY, RELAXATION & SPORT

HERE in Kent we have had our fair share of official royal visits. But members of the royal family have also chosen our county as a place to relax and enjoy themselves out of the public eye

And that has long been the case.

Queen Victoria holidayed in Kent as a child. Her second son, the Duke of Edinburgh, lived at Eastwell Park, Ashford, for many years. King Edward VII, George V and Edward VIII, later the Duke of Windsor, all played golf in Kent. The Duke of Kent is a Kent cricket fan.

Princess Anne's links with Kent go back to her classroom days when she became just another pupil of Benenden School – albeit one whose mother attracted rather more public attention than most.

The Queen and Prince Philip have enjoyed many relaxing visits to the home of Lord and Lady Brabourne, in Mersham, near Ashford, and have often been seen going to church together as a family on a Sunday morning. Prince Philip and Prince Charles have also both been regular guests at shooting parties there.

Perhaps it is not surprising that the two families are such firm friends since they are related through Lady Brabourne's father, Earl Mountbatten of Burma, who was both third cousin to the Queen and uncle to Prince Philip.

The family ties are close. The future Queen was a bridesmaid at the Brabournes' wedding in 1946.

She and Prince Philip are godparents to two of their sons and Prince Charles stood as godfather to their youngest sons, Timothy, and his twin, Nicholas, who died in the IRA bombing in Sligo in 1979 that also killed their grandfather, Earl Mountbatten, and their grandmother, the Dowager Lady Brabourne.

July 1904: King Edward VII made many visits to Eastwell House, Ashford, which for many years was the home of his brother, the Duke of Edinburgh. Picture: *E.D.Horn*

May 1928: The Prince of Wales, later King Edward VIII, regularly played golf at the Royal St George's Golf Club in Sandwich and even captained the club in 1927-28. Here he is seen presenting the Open Golf Championship to Walter Hagen. The club earned its royal title in 1902 from King Edward VII who also played there. Picture: *The Topical Press Agency*.

August 1949: The Duke of Edinburgh took to the field for Mersham-le-Hatch against Aldington while staying for the weekend with Lord and Lady Brabourne. Aldington batted first and were 29 for 4 when the Duke went on to bowl. He took three wickets for 27. But one of them, Frank Wanstall, took his revenge by getting the Duke out lbw for a duck on the first ball. The Hatch won by 118-79.

Princess Elizabeth and Lady Brabourne relaxed in deckchairs to watch the game.

June 1950: Children from Mersham and Brabourne Schools and the Caldecott Community had a grandstand view when Princess Elizabeth arrived at Mersham Parish Church to be godmother to Lord and Lady Brabourne's second son, Michael John Ulick. The service was conducted by the Archbishop of Canterbury, Dr Geoffrey Fisher.

October 1952: The Duke of Windsor played a round of golf with the Hon Patrick Davison at the Royal St George's Club, Sandwich, practising for the club's annual medal tournament the following day. He was staying at a hotel on the front at Sandwich Bay, where he hosted a dinner party for six golfing friends on the Saturday night.

October 1957: The Duke of Edinburgh went out shooting at Mersham-le-Hatch, while staying with Lord and Lady Brabourne.

April 1957: Just like any other family on a fun day out, the Queen and Duke of Edinburgh took their children, Prince Charles and Princess Anne, to the Romney, Hythe and Dymchurch Railway. Lady Brabourne is also in the picture.

December 1958: When the Queen and Duke of Edinburgh spent a weekend at Lord and Lady Brabourne's they would often be seen going to church with the family on Sunday morning. Here they are with their daughter Princess Anne and Lord and Lady Brabourne, leaving Smeeth Church with the Rector, the Rev O.W.Evans.

September 1963: The 13-year-old Princess Anne was one of 65 new girls at Benenden School. She arrived with The Queen and was introduced to the headmistress, Elizabeth Clarke. The Princess was 'mothered' by Elizabeth Somershield, who was the same age but in her second term. She was in Magnolia dormitory with three other girls.

Princess Anne was pictured on her first outing from Benenden on the Sunday after she arrived. She and her fellow pupils went to morning service at St George's Parish Church where the sermon was given by the Rev A.Jessop Price.

July 1964: The Queen made several visits to Benenden School while Princess Anne was a pupil. Here she and her daughter are seen enjoying each other's company at a garden party.

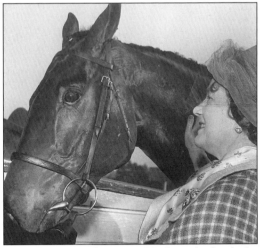

July 1964: Princess Anne took a jump on her horse, Jester, in the combined training competition at a gymkhana at Moat House, Benenden. She was a keen rider throughout her days at Benenden.

November 1964: The Queen Mother, who has had a lifelong interest in horse racing, has paid a number of visits to Folkestone Races. She made a surprise visit to a National Hunt meeting at which her horse, Arch Point, ridden by Bill Rees, won the opening race, the Marden Hurdle. Then Gay Record made it a double triumph for his royal owner when he won the Canterbury Chase, ridden by Bobby Beasley. "I've had a wonderful afternoon," the Queen Mother told people in the crowd. She is pictured with Gay Record.

July 1965: Princess Anne took part in an activity ride by pupils at Benenden School during a gymkhana open day. The girls all jumped while taking off their coats then while putting them back again. Earlier she had a clear round on her horse, Jester, in the Inter-School Show Jumping Contest. Benenden School came second in the contest.

The Princess took part in another fun event, The Nightmare, in which an old man in a white nightshirt lay asleep on an old bedstead in the middle of the arena, in what was supposedly a haunted house. The girls rode by and snatched off his night cap. Princess Anne donned a blue cloak and jumped clean over the bed.

April 1965: Prince Charles stood as godfather to Nicholas and Timothy, twin five-month-old sons of Lord and Lady Brabourne, at Mersham Church.

June 1967: Princess Anne relished her role as country yokel, Alfred, in Christopher Fry's short pastoral fantasy, *The Boy with A Cart*, performed at Benenden School speech day.

June 1968: Princess Anne again clearly enjoyed herself playing a drunken sailor in the chorus of Henry Purcell's opera, *Dido and Aeneas*, presented for speech day during her last term at Benenden.

July 1968: The Queen Mother, Princess Margaret, Richard Burton, Elizabeth Taylor, John Betjeman and Noel Coward were among the guests at the wedding of Sheran Cazalet, daughter of race-horse trainer Peter Cazalet, of Fairlawne, Shipbourne, near Tonbridge, and Simon Hornby of Berkshire, a director of WH Smith. The service, at Shipbourne Church, was conducted by the Archdeacon of Tonbridge, the Ven E.E.Maples Earle, who is seen here with the royal guests and the Rector of Frant, the Rev D.Berners-Wilson.

July 1968: Princess Anne was one of four pupils from Moat House Riding School who performed a quadrille to the music of Richard Strauss during Benenden village fête on Glebe Field. She wore a brocade Georgian coat, tricorn hat and grey wig.

July 1968: The Queen visited Benenden School on its annual hobbies day when she was taken on a high-speed tour of an exhibition of pupils' art, pottery, dressmaking and cookery. Her visit was also to mark the end of Princess Anne's five years at the school. After a buffet supper she watched the school play.

July 1968: Prince Charles drove to Brands Hatch in his blue MGC GT car, where he went to the Paddock and met some of the top Grand Prix stars including John Surtees, Graham Hill and Dennis Hulme. Also on the visit were the Duke of Kent and Lord Mountbatten, the chairman of the RAC.

That same weekend Prince Charles borrowed white shirt and flannels and a pair of size 10 boots to score 20 runs, including a six and two fours, in a charity cricket match at Mersham-le-Hatch. The game was between a Grand Prix drivers' team, captained by world champion Dennis Hulme, and a team organised by Lord Brabourne. Lord Brabourne's team won by 187 runs to 142. About 1,000 people watched the match which raised more than £400 for Springfield Boys' Club, the McIndoe Burns Unit at East Grinstead Hospital and the Grand Prix Medical Service.

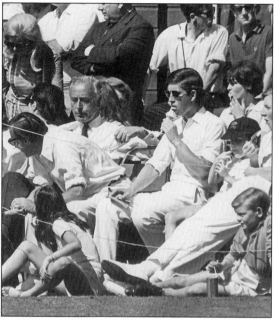

More action from the match between Dennis Hulme's team and Lord Brabourne's team. The Prince takes a run.

The Prince relaxing after his innings with his uncle, Lord Mountbatten.

August 1968: The Duke and Duchess of Kent had different loyalties when they lunched with Kent cricketers at the St Lawrence Ground in Canterbury during a Kent v Yorkshire match. It could have been a tense occasion for the Duke, patron of Kent County Cricket Club, and the Duchess, patron of Yorkshire County Cricket Club. In the end, the rain acted as peacemaker, ensuring that the game ended in a draw. The Kent captain, Colin Cowdrey, who was not playing because of an injury, introduced the Duchess to players and officials.

August 1968: Mother and daughter took a keen interest in Eridge Horse Trials. The Queen presented the trophies – including a rosette to Princess Anne who took fifth place in the class for novice under-21s.

April 1970: The Queen Mother enjoyed a joke with trainer Peter Cazalet at Folkestone Races. When his horse, Cloudsmere, won the Whitbread 'Elephant' Handicap Chase she handed him a bottle of County Ale as a token of the crates of beer due to the winning stable. Also in the picture is Lord Cornwallis, Lord Lieutenant of Kent.

September 1970: Princess Anne competed in the cross-country section of Knowlton Horse Trials at Knowlton Park, near Canterbury, on her horse, Purple Star.

December 1970: The Queen and her family visited Ashford Parish Church for morning service.

April 1971: The Duke of Kent was presented with two cricket bats for his sons when he and the Duchess joined the Kent County Cricket Club at a dinner in Maidstone to celebrate the previous season's victory.

August 1973: The Duke and Duchess of Kent visited Kent County Cricket Club's St Lawrence Ground at Canterbury to see a Kent v Yorkshire match. Captain Mike Denness presented his players to the Duke. From the left: Norman Graham, John Shepherd, Bob Woolmer, Graham Johnson, David Nicholls, Richard Elms, Asif Iqbal and Peter Topley.

September 1979: More than 500 mourners gathered at Mersham for the funeral of Doreen, Dowager Lady Brabourne, and her grandson, the Hon Nicholas Knatchbull, 14, who were both victims of an IRA bomb on board the family boat in Sligo, Eire. Earl Mountbatten of Burma also died, as did a schoolboy crew member. Lord and Lady Brabourne, and Nicholas's twin, Timothy, were injured in the attack and were still in hospital when the funeral took place. Among the wreaths left at the Brabourne family vault were two handwritten cards from the Queen and Prince Philip and one from Prince Charles to his godson, Nicholas. Prince Charles and Prince Philip were among the mourners at the funeral.

July 1980: Princess Margaret paid a flying visit to see her mother on board the Royal Yacht *Britannia* as it cruised past Gravesend taking the Queen Mother back to the Pool of London after an official visit to the Cinque Ports. The Princess arrived with her children, Lord Linley and Lady Sarah Armstrong Jones, at the Royal Terrace Pier in Gravesend where the Royal Barge was sent to pick them up.

The barge ferried them out to the Royal Yacht.

A winch was lowered to lift the barge out of the water to deck level so they could step on to *Britannia*.

November 1984: Cheering crowds lined the route to Ashford Parish Church hoping to catch sight of the royal guests at the wedding of Lady Joanna Knatchbull and Baron Hubert du Breuil of France. The Queen is seen leaving the church after the service flanked by two of her sons, Prince Charles and Prince Edward. Also among the 600 guests were Princess Margaret's son, Viscount Linley, his sister, Lady Sarah Armstrong Jones, The Queen of Greece and her daughter, Princess Alexia, Prince and Princess George of Hanover, the Princess of Hesse and the Rhine and Princess Andrew Romanoff.

July 1985: The Duke of Edinburgh went aboard one of the Tall Ships gathered at Chatham Dockyard for the 1985 Cutty Sark Tall Ships Race. As patron of the Sail Training Association he also made a point of visiting the STA's *Sir Winston Churchill*, crewed for this race by girls.

November 1986: Jockey Anne Phillips, alias Princess Anne, rode Glowing Promise in the 3.00 Leeds Amateur Riders' Stakes at Folkestone Racecourse. The bookies gave her odds of 8-1. She finished third, five lengths behind the winner, Galesa.

April 1989: The Princess of Wales brought her own charm to the wedding of her cousin Edward Berry, 28, to Joanna Leschalles, 29, of Cranbrook, youngest daughter of the former High Sheriff of Kent, Anthony Leschalles. The Princess stepped in to arrange the bride's train for the photographs outside St Dunstan's Church, Cranbrook. The five page boys included the young Princes William and Harry.

July 1993: The Duke of York relaxed in the crowds watching the 1993 Open Golf Championship at Royal St George's, Sandwich. It was won that year by Greg Norman.

August 1993: Prince Harry was delighted to be presented with a trophy from Formula One racing driver Johnny Herbert at the karting track at Buckmore Park, Chatham. He was applauded by his brother, Prince William, and his mother, the Princess of Wales, who is seen here with her back to the camera. Picture: *Press Association, John Stillwell.*

CELEBRATION
AND MOURNING

WHEN Diana, Princess of Wales died in August 1997 the people of Kent joined the rest of the nation in an extraordinary outpouring of sorrow. Yet this public demonstration of grief was by no means unprecedented.

The news of Queen Victoria's death in 1901 reached Kent by telegram and was announced to people who had gathered in town centres for information in those pre-broadcasting days.

Immediately all public functions were cancelled.

In Hythe the Town Band played the Dead March in the High Street. In Faversham the Carnival Club's annual smoking concert was abandoned.

Maidstone's Mayor told people to wear mourning and to keep their house blinds drawn until after the funeral.

The display of grief was formal and respectful.

Some Kent vicars argued in 1911 that King George V's Coronation should be treated similarly – as a religious ceremony not an excuse for jollifications.

But the people thought otherwise. There were fêtes and pageants in many Kent towns and a coronation exhibition in Ashford; 42 gallons of paraffin were used to light a 32ft high bonfire on Windmill Hill, Gravesend.

For King George VI's Coronation in 1937 Hildenborough residents were given free beer; the Mayor of Canterbury gave three pennies to every schoolchild; a flying display in Folkestone featured a mock air-raid on the town.

In 1953 everyone wanted to see Queen Elizabeth II's Coronation on the television. But afterwards people went out to have fun – at pageants, tea parties, concerts and firework displays. A baby born in Bearsted on Coronation Day was immediately wrapped in a Union Jack by a patriotic midwife.

The celebrations continued in 1977 for the Queen's Silver Jubilee when street parties were held in most Kent roads.

And in 1981 the county succumbed to wedding fever when Prince Charles married Lady Diana Spencer. It was a public holiday and everyone joined in the fun.

The Diana phenomenon, which would manifest itself so potently on her death, had already begun to take hold.

1895: When royal visitors arrived at Gravesend by boat they landed at Royal Terrace Pier. This archway was erected in welcome.

1895: This triumphal archway was erected in New Road, Gravesend, to mark a visit by Princess Henry of Battenberg to open the Technical Institute in Darnley Road.

January 1901: The people of Maidstone laid wreaths on the statue of Queen Victoria in the High Street on hearing of her death. Ninety-six years later they would again lay flowers round the statue, this time to mourn the death of Diana, Princess of Wales.

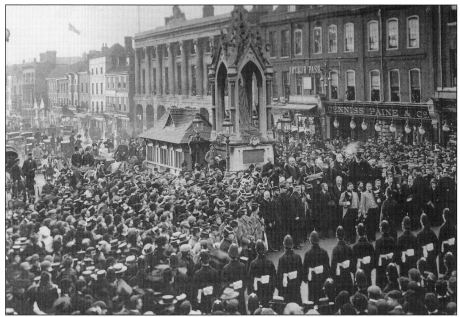

The monument to Queen Victoria towered over the people gathered in Maidstone to hear the Mayor read the proclamation of the accession of her son, King Edward VII, to the throne.

May 1910: The Mayor of Canterbury drove round the city to proclaim the accession of King George V. He paused by Canterbury East Station and stood up in his carriage to read the proclamation. Members of the City Corporation were in another carriage close by. The 21st Lancers lined the streets.

June 1911: A parade to celebrate the Coronation of King George V made its way through the streets of Tenterden.

May 1935: Celebrations were held throughout the country to celebrate the Silver Jubilee of King George V and Queen Mary. A thanksgiving service was held in the grounds of Tonbridge Castle.

The main gate at Chatham Dockyard was decorated for the festivities.

January 1936: Just a few months later the old King was dead and his eldest son ascended the throne for his brief reign as King Edward VIII. The ancient Burghmote Horn was sounded by the Town Sergeant and the proclamation declaring Edward VIII King was read outside the Old Guildhall, High Street, Canterbury.

May 1937: Maidstone was lit up in loyal celebration for the Coronation of King George VI.

February 1952: It was a solemn occasion in Maidstone when the civic party, led by the Mayor, Alderman B.J.Watson, assembled outside the Town Hall for the proclamation of Queen Elizabeth II.

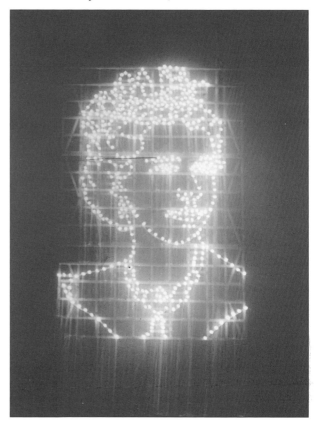

June 1953: This picture of The Queen lit up Mote Park, Maidstone, in celebration of the Coronation of Queen Elizabeth II.

The youngsters of Perryfield Street, Maidstone, sat down to a slap up tea as part of their Coronation celebrations.

Hundreds of children enjoyed this party at Richmond Road School, Gillingham, in celebration of the Coronation of Queen Elizabeth II.

May 1960: Crowds packed the promenade at Gravesend, which was decorated from end to end with bunting, to watch the Royal Yacht *Britannia* pass, carrying the newly-weds Princess Margaret and Anthony Armstrong-Jones off to their honeymoon in the Caribbean. Long before *Britannia* came into view ships' hooters up-river gave the signal she was on her way. Sea Rangers on Gravesend Customs jetty sent a message 'Good luck, God speed' with semaphore flags and received a thank you in reply from *Britannia*. At Greenhithe, more than 4,000 sightseers turned out to see the Royal Yacht. The 250 cadets on HMS *Worcester*, the Thames Nautical Training College ship manned the vessel and gave three cheers for the newly-weds. A message of good wishes was flashed out to the *Britannia*.

June 1977: The children of Alma Street, Sheerness, celebrated the Queen's Silver Jubilee with a street party.

Florist Gloria Moynes, of Rainham, made this blooming tribute to celebrate the Queen's Silver Jubilee. Her red, white and blue crown contained almost 100 flowers.

September 1997: Kent joined the rest of the country in grief at the sudden death of Diana, Princess of Wales. Flowers were laid at churches, monuments, war memorials and other places in memory of the Princess. The tributes at Canterbury Cathedral were laid out in the shape of a giant cross.